Bill Taylor, born in Birkenhead, Merseyside has visited Greece compulsively over a period of more than twenty-five years, including five overland journeys. Travels to the tropics, Africa, North America, Western Asia and the Far East have not diminished his enthusiasm for things Hellenic.

As a head of geology and geography departments in grammar and comprehensive schools over many years, Bill Taylor brings an insight into the physical make up of the country to blend with his affection for the Greeks and their way of life.

He is married with one son and lives on the Wirral.

To my mother
Smaller than average
but larger than life.

Greek Island Series
The Central Cyclades
Bill Taylor

Mykonos · Delos · Naxos
Paros · Antiparos

Roger Lascelles, Cartographic and Travel Publisher
47 York Road, Brentford, Middlesex TW8 0QP Telephone: 01-847 0935

Publication Data

Title	The Central Cyclades
Typeface	Phototypeset in Compugraphic Times
Photographs	Bill Taylor
Printing	Kelso Graphics, Kelso, Scotland.
ISBN	0 903909 60 X
Edition	This first September, 1987
Publisher	Roger Lascelles
	47 York Road, Brentford, Middlesex, TW8 0QP.
Copyright	Bill Taylor

Distribution

Africa:	South Africa —	Faradawn, Box 17161, Hillbrow 2038
Americas:	Canada —	International Travel Maps & Books, P.O. Box 2290, Vancouver BC V6B 3W5.
	U.S.A. —	Hunter Publishing Inc, 155 Riverside Dr, New York NY 10024 (212) 595 8933
Asia:	Hong Kong —	The Book Society, G.P.O. Box 7804, Hong Kong 5-241901
	India —	English Book Store, 17-L Connaught Circus/P.O. Box 328, New Delhi 110 001
	Singapore —	Graham Brash Pte Ltd., 36-C Prinsep St.
Australasia	Australia —	Rex Publications, 413 Pacific Highway, Artarmon NSW 2064. 428 3566
	New Zealand —	Enquiries invited.
Europe:	Belgium —	Brussels - Peuples et Continents
	Germany —	Available through major booksellers with good foreign travel sections
	GB/Ireland —	Available through all booksellers with good foreign travel sections.
	Italy —	Libreria dell'Automobile, Milano
	Netherlands —	Nilsson & Lamm BV, Weesp
	Denmark —	Copenhagen - Arnold Busck, G.E.C. Gad, Boghallen, G.E.C. Gad
	Finland —	Helsinki — Akateeminen Kirjakauppa
	Norway —	Oslo - Arne Gimnes/J.G. Tanum
	Sweden —	Stockholm/Esselte, Akademi Bokhandel, Fritzes, Hedengrens. Gothenburg/Gumperts, Esselte Lund/Gleerupska
	Switzerland —	Basel/Bider: Berne/Atlas; Geneve/Artou; Lausanne/Artou: Zurich/Travel Bookshop

Contents

Part 1: Planning Your Holiday

1 Introducing the central Cyclades islands
Mykonos 10 — Delos 10 — Naxos 11 —
Paros 11 — Antiparos 12

2 The climate of the Cyclades
Winter 13 — Summer 16 — Rainfall 17 —
Sunshine 18

3 Getting there
By air 22 — By rail to the mainland 24 —
By bus to the mainland 24 — By road to the
mainland 24 — Ferry services 26
Island hopping possibilities 28

4 Accommodation
Hotels, villas and apartments 32 — Rooms 33
— Camping 33 — Impromptu arrangements 34

5 Wining and dining
What to eat and when 36 — Eating places 37 —
The range of drinks 39 — Entertainment 41

6 Banks, shopping and the like
Currency 43 — Banks 44 — Post offices 44 —
Telephone services 45 — Ticket agents 45 —
Shops 45 — Hire of transport 46

Part 2: The Central Cyclades Islands

7 History in brief
Chronological events 48

8 Mykonos
Historical background 52 — Mykonos town 54
— Ornos, Psarou and Plati Yialos 62 —
Paradise and Super Paradise 64 — Agrari and
Elia 65 — Kalo Livadi 66 — Agia Anna Bay
and Kalafatis 68 — The north coast beaches 68
— Ano Mera 69 — The northwest coast 70 —
Accommodation 72 — Eating out 73 —
Mykonos bars 75

9 Delos
Background to Delos 81 — Mount Kynthos 82
— To the north of the harbour 82 — To the
south of the harbour 86 — Accommodation 88

10 Naxos
Naxos town 89 — Agios Prokopios and Agia
Anna 102 — Heading south: Naxos to Pyrgaki
106 — Apollona via Chalkio, Filoti and
Apiranthos 114 — Sidetracks to Moutsouna and
Lionas 124 — Accommodation 131 — Eating
out 131

11 Paros
Paroikia 141 — Naoussa and the north 149 —
Central Paros 160 — Southern Paros 167 —
Accommodation 177 — Eating out 179

12 Antiparos
Antiparos town and environs 187 — The cave
188
— Agios Georgios 190 — Accommodation 190

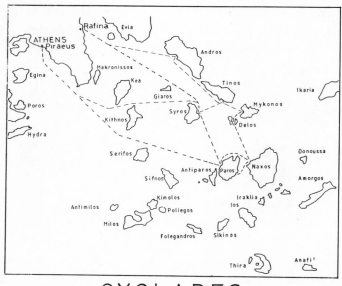

CYCLADES

ONE

Introducing the central Cyclades islands

The sea is an intrinsic part of Greece. The land is peninsular and insular, penetrated by the sea from all sides. The ramifying peninsulas and islands are separated by a variety of bays, gulfs and channels, some shallow and some deep. No place is far from water. It exerts its influence on many aspects of Greek landscape and life. The climate, vegetation and cultivation of the land are partly dependent upon the effects of the sea. The people have come to rely on it not only as a source of food but as an essential transport medium.

While the sea has separated Britain from the continent of Europe over the centuries, it has linked the myriads of islands and islets of Greece. The people have relied upon it, have endeavoured to master it, from the time of Odysseus to the present. Their success has been reflected in the size of the Greek merchant marine and the operations of shipping magnates like Onassis and Niarchos. Economic circumstances in recent years have diminished the significance of the Greek fleet. Vast numbers of ships are mothballed and rusting at various points around the coast but one thing that has not changed is the intricate network of ferries, large and small, that thread their way across the sea to provide the vital links for the islands. One of the most exciting prospects is the rush of vessels to and from the port of Piraeus during the summer months.

Greece has two major limbs of the Mediterranean around its shores. To the west the Ionian Sea incorporates islands that are generally green and pleasant. To the east the Aegean is studded with a host of islands of great diversity and separated by considerable stretches of water. Some islands are little more than a stone's throw from the mainland but others are nearly twenty-four hours' sail away.

Homer described the Aegean as the 'wine dark sea'. He may

have used a little poetic imagination but the sea is dark and commonly turbulent, raked as it is by the north winds. What many imagine as calm and blue water in reality is frequently ploughed and furrowed by white horses. Journeys may be scorching and placid but they are just as likely to be swaying, juddering experiences, unsettling to those of queasy disposition and best approached in a horizontal position.

Set within this basin to the east and southeast of Athens lie the Cyclades, a widely dispersed group of islands of singular character and marking the marine connection between the Pindos mountains of mainland Greece and the Taurus mountains of Asia Minor. Although they form a group, not all the islands are readily accessible from one another. Much depends upon the services which emerge from Piraeus. These tend to link islands together in chains while other connections may or may not exist.

Places often take their character from the structures and rocks of which they are formed. Many Aegean islands are of limestone and sandstone but in the central Cyclades the foundation material is a complex of granites formed in a molten state at considerable depth. These fluid rocks have emitted immense heat to bake others around them and the result is a landscape on its own. It is this individuality that has made the group a legendary attraction in the past and continues to draw visitors here in the present.

Mykonos

Mykonos is a small island but it embodies everything that has made the Cyclades a legend throughout the world. Bare hills under a blue sky, white cubic houses and round tower windmills with triangular cloth sails are images of an idyllic setting. The town is an intricate mesh of narrow alleyways between brilliant whitewashed walls. Coloured balustrades, gnarled doors, red-domed chapels and flourishing plants trailing from every window add to the picture.

The setting has attracted even more colourful summer inhabitants. Restaurants, cafés and bars have been developed with a flair and style to match the influx and to encourage it. Its coastline and its beaches are superb. Mykonos is small but it is beautiful.

Delos

Delos lacks both an indigenous population of fishermen and

farmers and a seasonal one of summer residents. Its origins are clouded in mythology and its development has been based upon its significance as a religious centre for the worship of Apollo. A checkered history has seen its vast store of architectural treasures laid waste, a grand jigsaw for French archaeologists to piece together. This has created an island of mystery with just enough revealed to stir the interest of all and to encourage a regular flow of daily visitors from Mykonos and, less frequently, from Naxos. It was a Sanctuary for Apollo in the past and it is an uncontaminated sanctuary of classical culture today.

Naxos

It is the largest and most compact island of the group. Its mountains reach 1,000 metres and are gashed by deep ravines and green valleys. The island is agriculturally productive but it also has areas that are wild and inaccessible. The coast has magnificent rocky sections and some of the largest and most beautiful beaches. The town of Naxos has a traditional *chora* of never ending interest and many rural villages, large and small.

Archaeological remains are not numerous but those that exist are striking. Every visitor is, in fact, greeted by the gateway to the Temple of Apollo, a giant white arch on the Palateia islet at the entrance to the harbour.

Perhaps the greatest virtue of Naxos is its Greekness. It has not been swamped by the tide of tourists but springs to life with its summer injection of Athenians. Naxos is not for instant holiday packages on a large scale but it is for selective and discerning people.

Paros

A little less than half the size of Naxos, Paros is another compact, circular island. It lacks the rugged, massive landscape of its larger neighbour but has in its place softer glowing yellow hills speckled with the white boxes of Cycladic architecture. Its villages are dispersed across the central uplands but are also spaced out along its coast. The *chora* of Paroikia, charmingly decked with basil, bougainvillea and geraniums, is a pearl matched by the little port of Naoussa on the northern coast.

The economy of Paros is rural but is rapidly changing as its attractions are transmitted abroad.

Antiparos

Very close to the Western shores of Paros is the slim form of Antiparos, a ridge of limestone in contrast to its granite partner. Its shrubby hills sweep down to a fretted coastline with small pockets of sand. The flanks of the ridge have few dwellings and most people live near the northern point of the island in the town of Antiparos.

A quiet island away from the bustle of Paroikia, this is the place for those seeking solitude and those who flock to see its cave, rendered famous by the graffiti of ages, as well as its mighty stalagmites and stalactites.

TWO

The climate of the Cyclades

Perhaps the weather is less important to visitors to Greece than it is to those heading for the Costa del Sol and Majorca. Greece offers rather more than enticing weather in the form of landscape, archaeological remains, architecture, culture and the way of life of the people. Weather, however, affects everyone and adverse conditions do not add to the enjoyment of any place.

Greece is, climatically, not a place for all seasons, a fact which is recognised by the closure of most facilities at the end of the last week in October; there is a grand reopening at Easter, or even a little later. But Athens and the nearby archaeological sites could readily be visited even in mid-winter.

Winter

Winter poses two weather problems to travellers. The first is the passage of depressions through the Mediterranean from west to east. In winter the sea is a pool of warmth which attracts the depressions and with them the humid air from the Atlantic. The result is a rainy winter. Travel in the months of November, December, January and February is likely to be interspersed with rain and even October and March are months in which wet days are a distinct possibility. In summer these depressions track farther north having been blocked by high pressure in the western Mediterranean. Figure 1 shows the pattern of rainfall for Athens and Mykonos.

The second adverse effect is the influence that the depressions exert on the flow of air into Greece. All depressions suck in air with a spiral motion rather like water descending a plug hole. As the air is pulled in from different points of the compass so the temperature conditions change and are very variable just as they

13

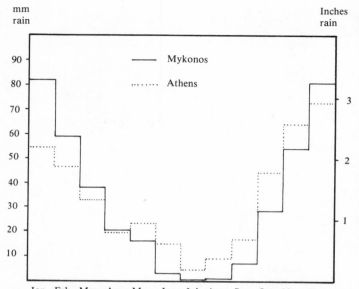

Figure 1   Average monthly rainfall in Mykonos and Athens

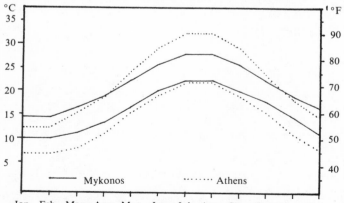

Figure 2   Average maximum and minimum temperatures in Mykonos and Athens

14

are in the British Isles. Commonly the wind drives down the Aegean Sea out of the centre of eastern Europe, which in winter is at or below freezing. These conditions become milder in their southward passage but still bring a cold blast to the islands in their path. Conditions are colder in Athens and other places on the mainland than they are in the islands, as is demonstrated in the graph (Figure 2). The central Cyclades in their mid-Aegean location benefit from the insulating blanket of sea which loses its heat slowly during the winter months. Thus in January Mykonos has a mean minimum temperature of 10°C (50°F). It also has a maximum of 14°C (58°F) indicating the variability at this season. There is little difference between the temperatures of individual islands though places on the northern windward side always appear cooler than in sheltered south-facing positions. Average monthly temperatures are shown for Mykonos, Naxos and Paros in Table 1.

Sea temperatures for Naxos are given in Table 2 and these demonstrate that swimming conditions are not simply tied to the seasons. Mid-winter and the shortest day in December do not occur in the middle of the off-season for swimming. It is possible to swim comfortably in sheltered conditions at least until the end of October and even into November because the sea cools down much more slowly than the air. On the other hand it warms up very slowly and the water is not enticing until about May. Even in high season swimming conditions can spring surprises. If the strong north wind, the *meltemi*, is blowing offshore as it commonly does on the southern beaches of Mykonos, it drives the warm surface water out to sea. In its place colder water wells up from the depths and can make swimming, even off the normally pleasant sandy beaches, a tingling experience. For comparison, the sea surface conditions on the sunny mid-Channel coast of Britain are provided as well as on the cooler North Sea. As can be seen, British sea temperatures do not peak until August or even September and they are still much lower than those of Naxos.

Summer

Summer in the Cyclades is another world. Its attractions are not limited to foreign visitors for there is also a mass exodus of Athenians to insular friends and relatives as well as to the host of villas, apartments and rooms. At least in part this is a climatic response.

Figure 2 shows that Athens has a mid-summer average maximum of 32°C (90°F) but bare statistics do not reveal all, climatically or figuratively. Averages, even maximum averages, do not indicate the extremes. Athens is set in a bowl below Mt Hymettus in which the heat builds up. It is compounded by the reflection and radiation from the pale buildings and pavements so that it seems unbearable. In contrast, the sea around the Cyclades does not reach such high temperatures and exerts this influence on the land. Naturally it is hot. Mykonos has an average maximum of 27.7°C (82°F) but lacks excessive peaks and is commonly swept by winds which give a freshness not necessarily evident in the figures.

	Jan	Feb	Mar	Apr	May	Jun	Jul	Aug	Sep	Oct	Nov	Dec	
Mykonos	12.2	12.2	13.3	16.6	20.0	23.3	24.4	24.4	23.3	20.0	16.6	14.4	°C
	54	54	56	62	68	74	76	76	74	68	62	58	°F
Naxos	12.3	12.3	13.9	16.4	19.3	22.8	24.7	24.7	23.1	20.2	16.9	14.1	°C
	54.1	54.1	57.0	61.5	66.7	73.0	76.4	76.4	73.5	68.3	62.4	57.3	°F
Paros	11.5	12.0	13.2	16.4	20.2	24.0	25.6	25.6	22.9	19.4	16.7	13.7	°C
	52.7	53.6	55.7	61.5	68.3	75.2	78.0	78.0	73.2	66.9	62.0	56.6	°F

Table 1   Average monthly temperatures in the central Cyclades

Month	Naxos °C	Naxos °F	Sandown °C	Sandown °F	Bridlington °C	Bridlington °F
Jan	14.3	57.7	9.0	48.2	6.0	42.8
Feb	14.3	57.7	7.0	44.6	5.5	41.9
Mar	14.4	57.9	7.2	44.9	5.7	42.2
Apr	16.1	61.0	7.7	45.8	6.7	44.0
May	18.3	64.9	10.2	50.3	8.5	47.3
Jun	20.7	69.2	13.0	55.4	11.2	52.1
Jul	23.3	73.9	15.2	59.3	13.2	55.7
Aug	21.8	71.2	16.5	61.7	14.0	57.2
Sep	21.4	70.5	16.7	62.0	13.5	56.3
Oct	19.9	67.8	14.7	58.4	12.5	54.5
Nov	17.0	62.6	11.7	53.0	9.2	48.5
Dec	15.3	59.9	9.5	49.1	7.2	44.9

Table 2 Comparing average sea surface temperatures in Britain and the central Cyclades

Rainfall

The rainfall graph (Figure 1) clearly indicates one of the most reliable features of Greek weather, namely the drought of summer. Rainfall is negligible during June, July and August, the total number of rainy days during these months averaging only three. Rainfall is still very light in April, May and September and prolonged rainfall is improbable. There is a slight difference between the mainland and the islands at this time. Athens is wetter because the intense heat induces convection to generate brief, if infrequent, thunderstorms. On the other hand Athens is drier in the winter as the winds frequently blow off the land. The lack of dense green cover in the Cyclades helps to maintain its aridity. The

17

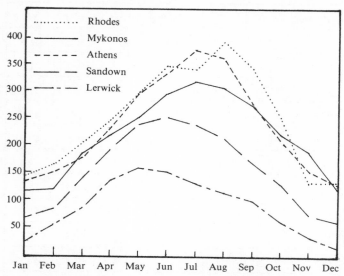

Sunshine
hours

.... Rhodes
——— Mykonos
– – – Athens
—— Sandown
—·—· Lerwick

Figure 3 **Comparison of monthly sunshine records in Britain and Greece**

ground is rocky or has dried yellow vegetation and this surface radiates heat, reducing the possibility of rainfall even if the air is moist enough. The total rainfall for Mykonos is 471.1 mm (19 ins) which is a little less than the driest place in the British Isles.

Sunshine

It follows that the lack of rain throughout the summer is associated with abundant hours of sunshine. In Athens the sunshine is offset by atmospheric pollution. Athens is one of the most rapidly growing cities in the western developed world and its blanket of smog, wedged between the enclosing hills, has been created by the combination of vehicle exhaust fumes, heavy industry, and dust rising from unsurfaced roads. In contrast the Cyclades are smog free as well as sunny.

Figure 3 shows the number of hours of sunshine received each

18

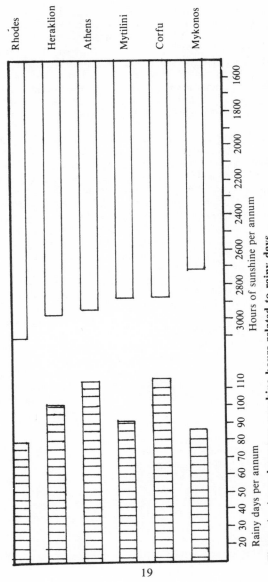

Figure 4 Annual average sunshine hours related to rainy days

19

month on Mykonos and other Greek locations. These peak in July or August. For comparison the British extremes are shown, Sandown in the Isle of Wight being the sunniest place in Britain. These graphs show that British locations are sunniest in June or even May and that there is a steady decline from that month onwards. It must be remembered also that an exaggerated view of British sunshine hours in summer is obtained because the total possible hours of daylight and sunshine is greater than in Greek latitudes: British evenings are protracted while the Greek twilight is brief.

The total number of sunshine hours recorded in Mykonos during the year, as well is in a number of other Greek and British locations, is shown in Figure 4. Most Grecian situations can be seen to receive 3000 hours of sunshine. In comparison British weather stations at low altitude record only half of that amount. The sunniest part of Britain lies along the southeast coast in Kent, Sussex and Hampshire with Sandown in the Isle of Wight receiving most with 1849 hours. One of the least sunny places in Britain, Lerwick in Shetland which has 1066 hours, is shown for comparison. Lower amounts of sunshine are found in many high mountainous regions and even in the Cyclades it is possible to see a cap of cloud hanging like a tablecloth over the peaks of Naxos. Fortunately it is there that the cloud stays. If it drifts off the highland it evaporates in the heat and the thermals of coastal regions.

The weather of Greece in summer is remarkably consistent. Its heat is very slightly tempered in the Cyclades but rain is a great rarity and the sun shines from dawn to dusk. For those who are able to visit before the high season, sunshine and dry conditions cannot be guaranteed but prolonged rain is improbable and spring brings the additional breathtaking bonus of a green sward over Paros, Mykonos and Delos, and a host of brilliant flowers.

THREE

Getting there

Only two of the islands — Mykonos and Paros — have airports though one is under construction on Naxos. There are no direct scheduled flights to Mykonos or Paros from the UK: you have to get to Athens first then take a domestic flight on Olympic Airways. Mykonos airport does, however, receive some direct international charter flights.

Ferries go regularly to Mykonos, Paros and Naxos from both Piraeus and Rafina. Delos is served only by the ferries from Mykonos or Naxos, and Antiparos is reached by ferry from Paros (Paroikia or Pounda).

Basically, then, getting to the central Cyclades islands described in this book involves a journey of two legs: getting to the Greek mainland and getting from the mainland departure point to the island of your choice. The main possibilities for the second

- **Mykonos** : By air from Athens
  By ferry from Piraeus or Rafina

- **Delos** : By ferry from Mykonos or Naxos

- **Naxos** : By ferry from Piraeus (via Paros) or Rafina
  (via Syros and Paros)

- **Paros** : By air from Athens
  By ferry from Piraeus or Rafina

- **Antiparos** : By ferry from Paros

Table 3   From the Greek mainland to the central Cyclades

leg are summarised in Table 3, but there are other ferry services operating between islands — see page 26.

By air

The airport is situated 10 km south of the centre at Elinco. Scheduled flights arrive from all over the world. From London (Heathrow) there are up to 25 per week. Flight time varies between 3½ and 4 hours for non-stop flights, more for those making an intermediate stop at Corfu and Thessaloniki.

Arriving by air

Athens airport has widely separated terminals for international traffic (eastern terminal) and for Olympic services (western terminal). In neither case is the terminal adequate. The larger international terminal has magnificent marble halls but was constructed in advance of the upsurge in Greek tourism and nightly charter flights. The result is grossly overworked bars and toilets, permanently full seats and floors covered by ruck-sacs, sleeping bags and bodies. Luggage laden travellers lined up at check points find other queues cutting across theirs in a bewildering melée while a sinuous thread of people weaves its way around the halls before slowly filtering through inadequate passport, customs and security facilities. Athens airport is a real deterrent to travel in Greece and one to be avoided where possible although as a connection to Piraeus it is vitally important.

Unfortunately the airport does not offer a regular or ready link to the port. Many travel companies provide a coach service but the individual traveller may have problems. The most obvious alternative is the abundant taxi service but be warned that many Athenian taxi drivers lack the charisma typical of the Greek people (though it would be harsh to tar all drivers with the same dubious character). Passengers faced by a barrage of Greek, excuses about an errant taximeter or reluctance to undertake a short journey, should examine their situation with caution.

As already stated, there are no regular scheduled services to the airports of the central Cyclades from Britain but, in recent years, Mykonos airport has been developed to take international charter flights. These operate from Gatwick and also from Birmingham and Manchester though these provincial airports may entail flight supplements (£12—£18 in 1987, according to season). The flight time is about 3¾ hours. Many reputable travel firms such as

Sunmed and Thomson use these services. Some travellers requiring more freedom in their selection of destinations choose to fly by charter to Athens and then move on from there.

Charter flight arrivals are expected to possess accommodation vouchers for the duration of their stay, these being issued by the company supplying the flight. These vouchers cover accommodation in hotels, villas, rented rooms and camping sites organised by the National Tourist Organisation. Vouchers are not needed on scheduled flights or on arrivals by train, coach, car or ferry.

It should also be remembered that anyone arriving from abroad with a passport bearing a stamp from the Turkish State of Cyprus or the Turkish Republic of Cyprus will not be granted entry into Greece and will be turned back at passport control.

Exiting on domestic air services

Olympic Airways, the domestic carrier, operates services to the central Cyclades which may suit those who are not partial to the longer sea journey. The fare structure is shown in Table 4. Return fares are double the single ones.

From	To	Single Fare (Jan 87)
Athens	Mykonos	£20.00
Athens	Paros	£21.00
Heraklion	Mykonos	£27.00
Rhodes	Mykonos	£29.00
Heraklion	Paros	£30.00
Rhodes	Paros	£34.00
Chios	Mykonos	£22.00
Samos	Mykonos	£20.00
Santorini	Mykonos	£15.00

Table 4   Domestic air services to the Cyclades

Only the services from Athens to Mykonos and Paros operate during the winter months using Short 330 and Dornier 228 aircraft respectively. The journey to Mykonos takes 50 minutes and that to Paros 45 minutes.

By rail to the mainland

Greece can be reached by rail from most European countries. This will usually involve joining one of three named expresses to Athens starting in northern Europe — the Venezia Express (dep Venice), the Hellas Express (dep Cologne), and the Akropolis Express (dep Munich).

Travellers from Britain, perhaps the principal users of this book, can connect with these trains. The cost of the ticket depends on whether the journey is via France, Belgium, or Holland (in order of increasing cost). Total journey time is of the order of 2½ days. Details from British Railways and their agents.

By bus to the mainland

The Europabus service, which is in fact owned by the rail companies of Europe, connects Athens with most of the countries of Western Europe. From London, the service leaves up to three times weekly, and takes 2½ days. Other buses, privately owned, also operate, but have been criticised in the past for inadequate safety standards.

Bus fares are cheaper than rail fares, except perhaps for those qualifying for concessionary rail fares.

By road to the mainland

There is no real difficulty in driving across Europe overland to Greece. The easiest route uses the (pay) motorway through Austria from Salzburg to Klagenfurt. The main *autoput* (M1/E94-E5) through Yugoslavia is joined between Klagenfurt and Ljubljana. It is a flat and uninteresting road and, because of its bad condition — especially north of Belgrade — and the large numbers of juggernauts using it, rather dangerous. However the proportion of the *autoput* reconstructed to full motorway standards increases every year.

The coast road down the Adriatic (M2/E27) is much more interesting, but 300 kms longer. Being slow and winding, it is also dangerous. It is not at present possible to transit through Albania. For political reasons there are sometimes restrictions on foreign motorists in Yugoslavia near the Albanian border.

Fuel coupons can be bought at the Yugoslav border. They must be paid for in foreign currency, and their cost is equivalent to a discount of 25% on the face value of the coupons. They are for use at any petrol station, to pay for all types of fuel. Unused coupons can be changed back for Yugoslav currency at the border, to show a small loss on the transaction.

An easier way of arriving in Greece is to drive into Italy and take one of the many car ferries available. Those sailing from the 'heel' of Italy (Apulia) would give the cheapest overall journey.

Documentation A 'Carnet de Passage en Douanes' is not necessary for periods of up to four months. Instead, an entry is made in the driver's passport. After four months, a banker's guarantee can be deposited as an alternative to the 'Carnet'. International Driving Permits are not needed by holders of British and some other European driving licences. An insurance Green Card, valid for Greece, is mandatory.

Fuel prices The price of Super petrol is comparable with other countries in the area. Diesel is much cheaper. Fuel prices vary slightly within the country depending on the distance from refineries. There is no price discounting. Currently, no tourist petrol coupons are available in Greece.

Motorways The 'motorway' network, called National Road, extends from Evzoni on the Yugoslav border to Athens. Most of it is still single carriageway, and there are even some sections of very ordinary main road. By convention, slower moving traffic drives on the hard shoulder. There are three toll sections between Evzoni and Athens — the first near Katerini. Charges are fairly modest. Tickets need to be kept for authentication within each toll section.

Road signs On the main roads, road signs invariably appear in pairs. The first gives placenames using the Greek alphabet, but this will be followed about 100 m after by a second using the roman alphabet. Other road signs conform to the normal European convention. Turnings off towards campsites are almost always signposted from the main road.

Breakdowns The Automobile and Touring Club of Greece (ELPA) operates a breakdown service in the less remote parts which is free to foreigners who are members of their National Automobile or Touring Club. Assistance is obtained by dialling 104.

Ferry services

Apart from the influx of tourists by international charter flights, most people will approach the central Cyclades by ferry. There are some inter-island ferries which do not touch upon the mainland but the majority of departures are from either Piraeus, south of Athens, or Rafina to the east of the city.

It is a curious fact that Piraeus, a port of almost perpetual activity, lacks both an organised connecting transport network and amenities for the vast throughput of ferry passengers. The ferries burst into life at 8 am with a flurry of departures. The hours leading up to this time are a salutary experience in island travel. Dawn breaks over one of the least salubrious collections of snack bars and toilets in Greece. Entertainment is provided by squadrons of stray dogs, rooting around and barking in frenzy at every arriving taxi. The advantage of enduring the hours before sailing is early embarkation of the ferry, a choice of deck space and the use of the toilet facilities before the hours of sailing render them untenable.

There is a considerable number of operators providing several ferries each day to the islands of Mykonos, Naxos and Paros. Tickets are available from an array of agents at the port. None offer cut-price tickets but fares are not excessive. Table 5a shows the fare structure in late 1986 from Piraeus.

From Piraeus to:	Car fares		Passenger fares		
	Max	Min	2nd Class	Tourist	3rd Class
Mykonos	No cars	No cars	£9	£7	£5.50
Naxos	£35	£20	£9	£7	£6
Paros	£35	£20	£9	£7	£5

Table 5a   Fare structure to central Cyclades from Piraeus

Piraeus has the advantage of a much greater number of ferries and routes and also the interest of a port with perpetual activity. On the other hand, Rafina is not a long bus ride out of Athens and it is a more pleasant point of departure than Piraeus. There are no striking economies to be made using the ferry from Rafina. Its fare structure (late 1986) is shown in Table 5b.

From Rafina to:	Car fares		Passenger fares
	Max	Min	One class
Mykonos	£33	£17	£6
Naxos	£34	£19	£6
Paros	£34	£19	£6

Table 5b   Fare structure to central Cyclades from Rafina

To some travellers an important consideration might be the length of the journey. The central Cyclades are not sufficiently distant to involve overnight travel though some vessels depart in late afternoon and arrive at night or in the early morning. Time on the water can bring the additional problem of sea sickness, a malady which is not precluded by an Aegean setting, especially when its surface is tormented by the *meltemi* winds. For uneasy travellers, Rafina has the advantage of offering a shorter journey by between an hour and two hours. Table 6 indicates approximate travel times but these vary with the vessel, the route taken and the weather encountered.

Port of departure	Destination	Duration of journey
Piraeus	Mykonos	6 hours
	Naxos	8 hours
	Paros	7 hours
Rafina	Mykonos	5 hours
	Naxos	6½ hours
	Paros	5 hours

Table 6   Approximate journey times to the central Cyclades

Some of the routes operating from Piraeus and Rafina terminate in ports of the central Cyclades but for some ferries these are just ports of call en route to more distant destinations. The advantage of this pattern is that it makes it possible to travel onward to other islands.

27

Island hopping possibilities

One of the most pleasurable features of Greek travel is island hopping. For many the stability of booked package tours is a prerequisite for travel, but for others the act of stepping on to a ferry bound for a previously untried destination with unknown accommodation changes a holiday into an adventure. Each 'hop' opens up new avenues of travel to other islands. If a landfall does not please, then the ticket agents await, surrounded by ship destination boards, beckoning travellers to a host of other possibilities. Each island in a chain connected by a ferry service can be explored in turn, providing scope for comparison and a ceaseless parade of the variety of Greece. Undoubtedly this is an opportunity to see all facets of the country and, because of the vast number of islands, it is a pleasure that can be protracted over a lifetime.

Table 7 indicates the ferry services and ports of call that are available from Piraeus. The times and vessels are subject to variations from week to week or even from day to day but the general pattern remains constant. No matter how up-to-date the timetable that is available, it is still essential to check times and ships at the port of embarkation.

Rafina cannot compete with this volume and variety of ferries. It has a daily service, departing at 07.45 and using the *Chrisi Ammos II,* to Mykonos calling in en route at Andros and Tinos. There is also a Sunday service by the *Chrisi Ammos III* to Syros, Paros and Naxos.

In June, July and August there is a daily ferry sailing from south to north through the central Cyclades and then returning in the late evening. This starts in Santorini at Thira, departing at 07.10 and calling in at Ios, Paros and Naxos on the way to Mykonos where it arrives at 15.20. The return journey begins at 16.20 but omits the call at Naxos and arrives at Santorini at 22.15.

One other major long distance service calling in at the central Cyclades is the twice weekly trip made by the *Nireas* from Rhodes to Piraeus. The route is indicated in Table 8.

Day	Time	Vessel	Ports of call
Daily	08.00	*Naias II* or *Panagia Tinou*	Syros, Tinos, Mykonos
Mon	08.00	*Naxos*	Paros, Naxos
	08.00	*Nereus*	Syros, Paros, Naxos, Ios, Santorini
Tue	08.00	*Naxos*	Syros, Paros, Naxos, Iraklia, Schinoussa, Koufonissia, Amorgos
	08.15	*Aegeon*	Paros, Ikaria, Samos
	08.45	*Georgios Express*	Tinos, Paros, Ios, Santorini
	12.00	*Santorini*	Syros, Paros, Naxos, Ios, Sikinos, Folegandros, Santorini, Anafi
	17.00	*Nereus*	Paros, Amorgos, Astypalea, Kalymos, Kos, Nissyros, Tilos, Symi
Wed	08.00	*Lemnos*	Paros, Naxos, Ios, Sikinos, Folegandros, Ia, Santorini
	08.45	*Georgios Express*	Paros, Ios, Santorini
Thu	08.00	*Naxos*	Paros, Naxos
	08.15	*Aegeon*	Paros, Ikaria, Samos
	08.45	*Georgios Express*	Paros, Ios, Santorini
	12.00	*Santorini*	Syros, Paros, Naxos, Donoussa, Katapola, Astypalea
Fri	08.00	*Lemnos*	Syros, Paros, Naxos, Ios, Ia, Santorini
	08.00	*Naxos*	Paros, Naxos
	17.00	*Georgios Express*	Syros, Mykonos, Paros, Ios, Ia, Santorini
Sat	08.00	*Naxos*	Paros, Naxos
	08.15	*Aegeon*	Paros, Ikaria, Samos
	12.00	*Santorini*	Syros, Paros, Naxos, Ios, Santorini, Anafi
	17.00	*Nereus*	Syros, Paros, Naxos, Iraklia, Schinoussa, Koufonissia, Amorgos, Astypalea, Donoussa
Sun	08.00	*Aegeon*	Paros, Ikaria, Samos
	08.00	*Lemnos*	Syros, Paros, Naxos, Ios, Ia, Santorini

Table 7   Daily ferry services from Piraeus to the central Cyclades

Day	Time	Vessel	Ports of call
Tue	20.00	*Nireas*	Karpathos, Kassos, Sitia, Agios Nikolaos, Santorini, Paros, Naxos, Piraeus
Thu	20.00	*Nireas*	Symi, Tilos, Nissyros, Kos, Kalymnos, Astypalea, Amorgos, Paros, Piraeus

Table 8   Rhodes to Piraeus ferry service

Within each island group there are many local ferry services which augment the major routes but are not widely advertised. Their operations are dependent upon weather conditions, demand and securing a licence. They include journeys between adjacent islands such as Paroikia and Pounda on Paros to Antiparos; Mykonos to Delos; and Naxos to Iraklia, Schinoussa, and Amorgos. These are usually carried out by smaller motor vessels designed for passengers. Most islands also have caiques or fishing boats which provide very regular services to the best beaches from a small jetty within the harbour. These are well advertised locally. If in doubt, follow the morning crowds.

It must be noted that it is not normally possible to book tickets for either passengers or vehicles on Greek ferries in advance from Britain. Tables at the end of the chapters on Mykonos, Naxos and Paros give full details of inter-island ferry services which can be booked on the spot if you decide to go in for the pleasure of island hopping once you are there.

Journeys by Greek inter-island ferries may not provide unmitigated pleasure but the passing hours are filled with a marvellous parade of humanity including Athenians, islanders and a largely youthful flood of north Europeans. The Greeks normally seek the shade and soft seats of the saloons in large numbers along with outsize and somewhat frail luggage. In contrast, the German, Swedish, Norwegian, Danish, Dutch, French and British passengers cannot get out on to the deck and into the sun fast enough. The movement of the ship coupled with the wind makes deck travel one of the most potent sources of sunburn even in Greece, guaranteed to etch out irremovable strap or sleeve marks on accumulating tans.

The reliability of the Greek ferry service is not fabled far afield. To some degree it is dependent on the size of the vessel and its ability to weather high seas. However, the major control is the *meltemi,* the strong northerly wind which rakes the Aegean sea for long periods. This is quite capable of curtailing the activities of smaller local ferries so that a precisely timetabled itinerary is a virtual impossibility. There is little point in relying on arrivals to the minute, to the hour or even to the day in order to make transport connections.

If island development is partly dependent upon available air services, then ferries make an even greater impact. Planes link a few islands but ferries reach out to all and large ships are capable of carrying much greater numbers. Here, the controlling factors are the size of the ferry and the frequency of services. If there are one, two or more ferries per day, then the island encourages tourism and progressive change takes place. If there is not a daily boat then package tourism is discouraged and the island remains Greek in character. Some islands such as Amorgos, Heraklia, Schinoussa, Anafi, Folegandros and Kassos are remote and have a very limited service. In consequence they are strikingly unaltered.

The Greek islands may be changing their traditional character with the advent of wide-ranging tourism but, hopefully, it will be a long time before the creeping corrosion affects all. For the devotees of Greece and its culture many possibilities remain but each year necessitates a greater effort to attain the idyll.

FOUR

Accommodation

The way in which accommodation has been expanded in the holiday centres of the Mediterranean may be a fair indication of the attitude of the government and the feelings of the people to the development of tourism. Greece, fortunately, has been conscious of its historical heritage as well as the attractions of its landscape. It has not permitted widespread replacement of natural assets by vast conventional resorts catering for package tours. There are resorts attached to modern built-up areas. Thus Vouglialmeni and Glyfada have grown on the fringe of Athens. In other cases areas of flat coastal land have been developed adjacent to airports such as Heraklion in Crete and modern Rhodes town. A few more attractive landscapes have been partially buried beneath concrete, plastic and glass as, for instance, at Agios Nikolaos in Crete and at many places on the coast of Corfu.

The blending of a tourist industry, essential for the economic future of many areas, with the conservation of the landscape is almost an impossibility but the central Cyclades have made a very reasonable attempt to achieve it. There are, it is true, very few large hotels. Only three have more than a hundred beds and those are all on Mykonos. The secret of success has been to construct buildings with a low, inconspicuous profile and in the cubic or rectilinear style traditional to the Cyclades.

Hotels, villas and apartments

Hotels are graded in these islands in categories from A to E. They are controlled by the National Tourist Organisation of Greece, who fix prices and determine classification. Only two hotels, the Ano Mera and Leto on Mykonos are in the A grade. There are none on Naxos, Paros, Antiparos or Delos but this does not mean that lesser grades are anything other than very acceptable. Details of hotel categories and accommodation are found at the end of each island section in Part 2. Bear in mind, however, that hotel accommodation is pre-booked by tour operators for the whole season and often is not available to the casual traveller.

In recent years there has been massive development of villas, apartments and rooms built specifically for the visitors from western Europe. These are simple but well appointed and rarely a disappointment.

Rooms

Perhaps the most desirable accommodation in many ways is in rooms provided by the people in their own houses. Travel companies have made inroads even here in more popular centres. It is still possible to obtain rooms, especially outside the high season, at the ferry arrival jetty. Greeks with rooms to let greet disembarking passengers with calls of *Domatia!* (Rooms!) It is possible to debate the price but there is little variation and the owners are not normally intent on ripping off the tourist. Similar accommodation may sometimes be obtained by walking up through the narrow ways of towns and villages enquiring about rooms. The advantage of using local rooms is that it gives an insight into the home and, above all, it brings the traveller into contact with the charming island people of Greece. A word here and a word there lead to a shared water melon or an ouzo together. Every word of Greek that is learned is repaid in the friendly contact that is made.

Camping

Camping provides the alternative accommodation for many but officially designated camp sites are few and far between and inevitably they are crowded. The result is that unofficial camp sites spring up everywhere. In some cases small ridge tents are pitched and, in others, impromptu shelters made from local canes are constructed like wigwams amid the sand. Attitudes to such activities vary. If there are complaints from locals about unsightly camps, fire hazards, disturbance of the peace or any one of a multitude of things then police arrive with a fourwheel drive vehicle to move people on. However, tourism is a livelihood and the police are not belligerent or looking for opportunities to harass the visiting youth.

It is, in fact, remarkable just how tolerant both the police and the people are to the life style of many visitors. No doubt it is this friendly and understanding attitude that makes Greece such an attraction.

The character of camping varies considerably. There are those who simply walk to the edge of the town and put their sleeping bags on the sand at the top of the beach beneath olives or tamarisks. Even within the town, beaches have a scattering of late arrivals. Those seeking more permanent quarters and the few who have brought their own transport move farther afield. Official sites simply do not exist to cope with the demand for places. People with motor caravans, vans and fourwheel drive pick-ups are commonly independent to a degree and can survive with few amenities for some time. They are fortunate to be able to choose some idyllic places such as the cape of Mikri Vigla on Naxos. Those with limited means and back packs can't afford to be too far from toilets, showers, eating and drinking facilities. Also, understandably, they tend to be gregarious. Part of their enjoyment of the setting is to share it with other people like themselves. Popular places in consequence are adjacent to tavernas on many of the smaller and more attractive beaches. Tavernas are anxious to maintain a population of dependent visitors for as long as possible and do not really want them to be moved on. Many provide a rudimentary shower for the benefit of campers.

Impromptu arrangements

Remember that those arriving on charter flights are supposed to be in possession of accommodation vouchers. If this were checked and enforced strictly or, indeed, if it were possible to do so, it would preclude unhindered travel to many visitors among the islands of Greece and this is not the idea of the legislation. One thing that it may do is to limit the influx of people into such a popular island as Mykonos where it is not difficult for accommodation to be completely filled. Unbooked visitors have been known to be stranded in their suits and dresses, along with stacked suitcases, looking for a night's resting place on the beach.

Many couriers operating with tour companies have extensive knowledge of rooms that may be available for the night and sometimes longer even on Mykonos. Their problems in transporting people between islands when ferries are cancelled or delayed make it necessary to have places they can fall back on. Their knowledge may well extend to several islands so that if impromptu arrangements are being made, it is well worth consulting a courier whether you have travelled with the company or not.

FIVE

Wining and dining

Greek food is not renowned throughout the world as a gourmet's delight. Neither are Greek restaurants temples to the pleasures of the palate but this does not mean that eating out need be anything other than enjoyable.

Many people have come to know Greek food through their local Greek restaurant in London, Birmingham, Manchester or Liverpool. The visit to such a restaurant may have preceded the first trip to Greece or it may have followed up a Greek experience. Commonly, the decor in a Greek restaurant in the U.K. is similar to what you find in Greece: the Greeks are not traditionally associated with splendour in restaurant decor. Rather their restaurants are utilitarian places of plastic and metal and could be regarded as plain or even tasteless. Conditions grow on one. What may seem ordinary initially, later becomes homely or even welcoming. Usually it is the scope of the menu that marks the main difference between Greek restaurants abroad and those in Greece, especially when the latter are set in small villages and ports in the islands. In Britain, the whole range of traditional Greek main course dishes may well be available as well as starters and possibly sweets. In the Greek islands, starters such as taramosalata and hummus are commonly missing and the main course range may offer little more than lamb or chicken, stuffed tomatoes and meat balls. There are, of course, many places offering much more than that.

What to eat and when

In Greece, where bed and breakfast terms are the exception, one of the ever-present pleasures is the saunter down to a *kafeneion* on the waterfront to partake of a leisurely coffee with toast and honey. Not too many people are set on a fry-up in the warmth and sunshine of Greece at the outset of the day. Each day it can be a different choice of venue from which to watch the world go by.

Some people literally make a meal of midday while others regard it as a minor intrusion into beach activity. The Greeks are liable to work through the menu and draw out the process into an afternoon siesta. The prospect of a hot meal does not appeal readily to all westerners, or at least not every day. The popular *horiátiki saláta* (that is 'Greek' salad of lettuce, onion rings, sliced peppers, black olives, olive oil with herbs and feta cheese) with *psaria* (fish such as whole grey mullet or red snapper) and *patátes* (chipped potatoes) can be enticing with a cold beer or retsina.

Whatever the attitude to lunch, the evening situation is a different one. Everyone wishes to spend time over dinner and looks forward with anticipation to the occasion. One of the most satisfying aspects of eating out in Greece is the open door to the kitchen. The inability of many to understand the menu, either in the original Greek or in the amusing translation which may be set out alongside, has helped to create the situation. The waiter invites inspection of the food being offered so that a name can be applied to each item. Nobody is self-conscious about cooking conditions. It is unbelievable that such a welcome could be extended into British kitchens.

A word of caution might be applied to the conclusions drawn from the inspection of food in the kitchens. Many of the dishes such as stuffed tomatoes, stuffed aubergines, beans with tomatoes, stuffed vine leaves and even chipped potatoes are prepared in advance. This means that when they are to be served they are cold. Only items which are to be cooked on ordering will actually be served hot. This will apply to fish, kebabs or anything put on to a charcoal grill. Cold dishes may be disappointing but it is difficult to persuade waiters or cooks to reheat food even with oft repeated cries of *poli zésti, efharistó* (very hot, please). It might be wise to choose definitely hot dishes or to ask whether they have a hot item. For example, *éhete, patátes polí zésti?* (have you hot chipped potatoes?)

Eating places

All eating places have the same function. The *kafeneíon* is for breakfasts, casual drinks, ice creams, coffee and similar items. A *zaharoplasteíon* may serve the same purpose but it specialises in sweets. The *estiatórion* is a restaurant serving lunch and dinner while a *tavérna* is an inn or eating house serving much the same function. A *psistariá* is a place specialising in hot grilled food.

An evening meal might begin at a *kafeneíon* for an aperitif ouzo, taken with *mezés* or *mezethákia* (snacks of peanuts, sunflower seeds and olives). There are *kafeneíon* with small charcoal grills cooking slices of octopus which can be bought as snacks for the same purpose, like those at the harbour in Naoussa on Paros and by the small jetty on the waterfront at Naxos.

The choice of *estiatórion* or *psistariá* is large in centres such as Paroikia, Naxos and Mykonos, and reasonable in resort villages such as Naoussa and Piso Livadi on Paros and Platis Yialos on Mykonos. Where there is variety it will include grills and restaurants serving traditional Greek meals and others which offer international cuisine as well as Greek food but at higher prices. There are foreign food bistros serving pizzas, pastas and risottos and some fast food or self-service cafeterias.

Except in a very few *estiatórion* and *tavérna,* there is not a wide choice of Greek dishes on the menu. Anything extraordinary will emerge from the deep freeze. Most restaurants serve standard products such as mousaka, stuffed tomatoes, peppers and aubergines and meat balls. Customers of limited means regard these as main course meals but more expensive restaurants can look askance at people ordering these items as anything other than starters.

The most common items found on menus appear in Table 9. Most waiters in main towns and resorts understand English but rural and isolated communities may speak only Greek. The table includes the Greek script for menu items and the approximate pronunciation. The critical feature of the pronunciation of Greek words is that the stress is placed on the correct syllable. This is, therefore, accented in the table. For example it is essential that the popular mince and aubergine pie is called *mousakás* and not mousáka, if it is to be understood.

Although there are restaurants which serve a sweet, Greeks commonly move on to a *kafeneíon* or *zaharoplasteíon* to complete their meal. These places cater for this specific need by providing coffees, alcohol, ice cream and a variety of sweet pastries. Their location is usually central to the action, an ideal place to watch the circulation of both Greeks and visitors around the town. All serve traditional Greek sweets, most of which tend to be very sweet indeed. The best known are *baklavá,* flaky pastry with chopped walnuts and almonds and coated in honey, and *halvas,* which is cinnamon-flavoured semolina and almond cake with lemon juice. Others include *katáifi,* a shredded wheat with nuts and honey, and *galaktobóureko,* which has flaky pastry around custard and syrup.

The range of drinks

One thing that helps to make eating enjoyable is the range of alcoholic drinks that Greece produces.

English beer buffs may not rate highly the produce of Greece; most commonly sold are Fix and Heinekens, both brewed in Greece. What does recommend them is that they are invariably served cold, which is an essential attribute in this climate.

The islands do not possess great areas of vineyards but some, like Paros, produce local wines which are mostly very reasonably priced. Light dry white wines are produced such as those under the label Demestica, and others having titles like Vulcano, giving a clue to their origin. Certainly most popular is the dry white retsina. Wines are supposed to have been resinated even in amphora dating back to the days of classical Greece. The resin gives the wine an exceptional dryness which critics dismiss as unpalatable turpentine. Travellers in Greece, however, usually come to the conclusion that very cold retsina is essential to complete the enjoyment of Greece. It is an acquired taste but once gained it is never lost. There are literally dozens of labels available, such as Plaka, Kourtaki, Marco and Patraiki. Most are from the mainland but some are from the islands, including Meltemi from Paros. All are different as the degree of resination varies. Retsina is normally taken to be a white wine but there are less common resinated red wines.

In contrast to the light dry and resinated white wines is Samos, derived from the island of that name. It is sweet, like liquid raisins, and extremely heady. One to beware of for the uninitiated.

Those visitors whose tastes have been cultivated on clarets and burgundies may find Greek reds not to their liking. Better quality reds like Danielis tend to be more expensive. Mavrodaphne, one of the more famous red wines, is surprisingly sweet.

Liqueurs and spirits are produced in quantity in Greece and are very cheap. Ouzo, the colourless aniseed spirit, is the most widely taken aperitif. It clouds with water or ice, like Pernod and Pastis. Again there are many labels and many qualities. All are not equally strong and, like retsina, ouzo tends to be an acquired taste.

There is a variety of other spirits. Kitron, a citrus liqueur, is

STARTERS & SALADS

πεπόνι	pepóni	melon
χυμός φρούτου	himós fróutos	fruit juice
ταραμοσαλάτα	taramosaláta	fish roe with olive oil
σατζίκι	tsatsíki	yoghurt, garlic, cucumber
χωριάτικη σαλάτα	horiátiki saláta	salad with feta cheese
μελιτζανοσαλάτα	melidzanosaláta	aubergine salad
ντολμάδες	dolmádes	stuffed vine leaves
μαρίδες	marídes	whitebait
ομελέττα	omelétta	omelet
αυγά σφικτά	avgá sfiktá	hard boiled eggs

MAIN COURSES

κεφτέδες	keftédes	meat balls
μουσακάς	mousakás	mousaka
γεμιστές ντομάτες	yemistés domátes	stuffed tomatoes
γεμιστές πιπεριές	yemistés piperiés	stuffed peppers
καλαμαράκια	kalamarákia	baby squid
μπαρμπούνι	barboúni	red mullet
ψάρι σχάρας	psári skáras	grilled fish
κοτόπουλο	kotópoulo	chicken
σουβλάκια	souvlákia	kebabs
αρνί	arní	lamb
αρνίσιες μπριζόλες	arnísies brizóles	lamb chops
χοιρινές μπριζόλες	hirinés brizóles	pork chops
φιλέτο σχάρας	filéto skáras	grilled steak
λουκάνικα	loukánika	sausages
πατάτες	patâtes	potatoes
φασολάκια	fasolákia	green beans

METHODS OF COOKING

στό φούρνο	stó fóurno	baked
βραστό	vrastó	boiled
ψητό	psitó	roast
τηγανιτό	tiganitó	fried

Table 9   Greek menu items

produced on Naxos. Another is Mastika, a colourless liqueur derived from the mastic gum trees of Chios, and Raki is produced on Ikaria. One of the most popular of spirits with its own distinctive taste is brandy. To the connoisseur brought up on the produce of the Cognac region of France, Greek brandy may not be in the same league. It is a darker, richer colour and has a much fruitier flavour than its French forbears. Grecian travellers are not prone to make comparisons with France. They are inclined to enjoy Greece for itself and a Metaxa brandy makes a fitting companion to a coffee at the end of the day.

Entertainment

The central Cyclades, indeed the majority of Greek islands, are not in the business of producing an array of entertainments. Those seeking casinos, theatres and a variety of performers to entertain them each night will no doubt find a 'costa' to suit them elsewhere. Essential to Greece is the ambience of eating and drinking in a place of character, in the country's inimitable style with interesting people, both local and foreign.

Almost always with any meal taped bouzouki music twinkles on in the background accompanying a plaintive folk song chanted by an urgent, pleading female voice. Gravelly toned men expound to the racing notes of the bouzouki on the heroic struggle for freedom and independence. *Agápi mou* (my love) is the theme for many haunting melodies. Greek music to the uninitiated, like that of the Arab world, resembles a cry from the heart, a rather sad and wailing record of past and present suffering. Eating and drinking in tavernas and cafés subjects the visitor to unwitting saturation in the musical culture of Greece. What starts out to the western ear as a slightly discordant noise develops into a foot-tapping rhythm and then into a mind-filling theme tune. The words may be meaningless but they seem apt and memorable. It is but a short step to securing tapes with the voices of Maria Farandouri, Haris Alexiou, Anna Vissy or Nana Mouskouri and the music of Mikis Theodorakis.

There is an image of Greek tavernas inhabited by a clientele of aged Zorbas, all biding their time before breaking into a spontaneous dance to the accompaniment of smashing plates. Real life is not like that even off the beaten track. On religious festival days things do happen. People flock into the towns and villages from the countryside and music, singing and dancing may follow.

To benefit from this it is necessary to find out local saints' days and to know the village where each day is celebrated. Usually transport is laid on to carry participants to the occasion. The roads are jammed and seats in the tavernas are at a premium in these locations.

In the more popular tourist towns like Mykonos, then taverna dancing may be a regular occurrence in which visitors participate. However, this bears little resemblance to a Greek celebration and is no more spontaneous than an outbreak of flamenco dancing on the Costa del Sol. It will hardly be a memorable occasion and does little to enhance the aura of Greece. Naturally there are exceptions and well known groups of musicians and dancers do appear in Mykonos and Paroikia to demonstrate their skills.

Entertainment in the central Cyclades is normally of a very limited nature but Mykonos is cosmopolitan. All levels of income are represented in its summer population and all manner of tastes are present among them. A large number of visitors are youthful and there are many bars and discos providing the necessary output of loud pop music. Because all tastes are found, other bars specialise in classical music or emit quiet, melodious ballads for more intimate tête-a-têtes. As a considerable number of visitors to Mykonos are 'gay', many places cater for their tastes. Entertainment is available that owes nothing to Greece in its origins and ranges from drag acts to striptease. As has been emphasised, the Greeks are remarkably tolerant but this does not preclude the police from making visits to some of the establishments in Mykonos town on occasions.

For those with more moderate tastes Mykonos possesses two cinemas, the Leto and the Artemis, the programmes of which are usually broadly advertised around the harbour. Some Greek films are shown and many out-of-date English language ones.

SIX

Banks, shopping and the like

Currency

There are restrictions which limit the issue of Greek currency abroad to 3000 drachmae per person which, depending on the current rate of exchange (207 drachmae = £1 in March 1987) may be as little as £15. This ensures that visitors must take in foreign currency on which there are no restrictions, or travellers cheques. It also means that the rate of exchange in Greece is the rate at which drachmae are available, and this is considerably lower than the figure quoted in Britain or in other western nations.

The drachma has been slowly but steadily devaluing relative to other major currencies in recent years. After a long period of stability the rate slumped from 100 to 230 drachmae to the pound in 1985 and the economy does not suggest that radical changes are imminent. Values of Greek notes and coins in circulation are shown in Table 10. Smaller units such as 1 drachma and subdivisions of the drachma, the leptae, are virtually valueless.

Notes	Coins
1000 drachmae	20 drachmae
500 drachmae	10 drachmae
100 drachmae	5 drachmae
50 drachmae	1 drachma

Table 10   Greek notes and coins in circulation

43

Banks

It must be remembered that banks are closed on Sundays and it may be difficult or impossible to exchange money or cheques. On other days banks are normally open from 08.00 until 13.00. Like many other establishments they are closed during the afternoon siesta.

The problem with banks is that they are few and far between and they are therefore grossly overworked. Very large queues build up, which irritate and frustrate the visitor. Each transaction is a two-part affair involving first the bank clerk and then a move to the cashier. There is no way round the problem except to be at the bank early, that is at opening time. Even then people are likely to be waiting.

Banks are located only in the main towns of Mykonos, Paroikia and Naxos. All are located on, or very close to, the waterfront. There are normally two, the National Bank of Greece and the Commercial Bank but there may be a third, such as the Agrarian Bank in Naxos. Your choice of bank is immaterial: all are busy.

Post offices

Post offices *(tachidromío,* with the 'ch' pronounced as in the Scottish loch and the emphasis definitely on the final 'i') open at 08.00 but tend to have longer hours than banks, closing at noon and reopening in the evening from 16.00 until 19.00.

Stamps are called *ta grammatósima* and are sold not only in post offices but also in the little kiosks found on the waterfronts. The convenience of purchasing them there outweighs the slight extra charge which they may make for the service. Post boxes are neither numerous nor obvious. They are usually attached to walls and are painted yellow.

Post offices are not always as easily found as one might anticipate though they are centrally placed in the main towns. In Mykonos, the post office is located in the block beside the 'Mykonos Hilton' beach and the Polikandrioti waterfront. In Paroikia, it lies a very short distance inland from the waterfront windmill just behind the white and blue chapel of Agios Nikolaos. Naxos has its office tucked away in a road running off the Filoti to Apollona route, close to the National Bank and parallel to the sea.

One of the useful services provided by the Post Office for people who are travelling without predetermined addresses is to act as collecting stations for mail. Letters sent poste restante to a particular post office will be held for up to three months awaiting collection by the traveller on production of proof of identity.

Telephone services

The initial letters O.T.E. signal the location of the telephone service for those wishing to call home. In some cases it is possible to call direct using the 0044 code for the United Kingdom but generally the lines are extremely busy and there may be a considerable delay in making a call after booking it. The experience may be more frustrating than cashing money at the bank. Normally the operator directs the caller to a numbered box when the connection is made. The call is metered and paid for on completion.

Ticket agents

There is little problem in obtaining tickets or information about inter-island travel. There are several agencies in Paroikia, Mykonos and Naxos. Naturally they are located on the waterfront and harbour and in all English is spoken. Tickets are readily available for all sailings and every departure is clearly outlined on blackboards and posters outside the office. These detail the sailings by days indicating the name of the vessel departing on each day, the ports of call being made and the time of departure. The same offices usually supply tickets for excursions by coach to local resorts, villages and archaeological sites though many local ferries to beaches on all the islands are paid for on the ferry itself after departure.

Shops

Shopping hours are ill-defined in resort towns. They are likely to be open at all hours whereas in other villages and towns, they close at midday and reopen at 17.00. Closing time depends upon trade.

Mykonos possesses exclusive and specialist shops for gold, silver, jewellery, fashion clothes and leather goods. Many of these items are very expensive but locally crafted silverware such as rings and bangles can be both attractive and reasonable. Silversmiths will make alterations to suit individual requirements on the spot. Skilled

45

smiths are also to be found in Naxos and Paroikia. Leather goods offer an attractive buy. There is a vast collection of satchels, grips, money pouches, handbags, belts, hats and jackets, largely in tan shades.

Each port is equipped with a good book store supplying a variety of paperbacks in English, French and German. They also have numerous maps, booklets and photographic volumes about the islands and archaeological sites. In addition they supply foreign language newspapers for those who do not like to be too far away from the cricket scores. The papers will probably be one day out of date and will be quite expensive.

There are one or two supermarkets in the main towns which offer a staggering variety of foodstuffs from feta cheese to cornflakes. There are masses of tinned goods, both Greek and imported but the latter tend to be dear and are to be avoided.

Mykonos is not endowed with great agricultural resources in the way that Paros and Naxos are so fruit and vegetables have to be brought in from the mainland. Elsewhere fruit and vegetable shops are very variable in quality but the good ones are a pleasure to the eye and to the camera.

Hire of transport

A phenomenon which has developed very rapidly in recent years is the opening of places hiring bicycles, mopeds, motor bikes, cars and jeeps. Hired motor cars are not cheap in Greece but push-bikes and mopeds represent good value as they are inexpensive and they do open up less accessible places for exploration. Motor bike licences and hard hats are not insisted upon in many places and this may lead to misguided use of the larger machines. A deposit will have to be paid and the hirer may have to surrender his or her passport as a guarantee. The major towns all have a number of hiring places and, on Paros, smaller resort villages also offer bicycles and motor bikes.

SEVEN

History in brief

The Cyclades islands are scattered across the Aegean. Their widespread distribution left them open to settlement and control by various city states of Greece as well as by external forces. Similarly, those administering them were faced with the impossible task of maintaining control. Rule changed hands at regular intervals but prosperity and growth occurred during longer periods of stability under the Athenians and Romans and, later, the Venetians. Even at these times the sequence of events is rendered complex by constant struggles for power and by external forces involving the Persians and Spartans.

After the strength of Roman rule, the islands were open to devastation by marauding pirates and a multitude of invading forces. The Dark Ages is a term which may be aptly applied to this period in the Cyclades as the cultural achievements of preceding eras were erased again and again. Goths, Vandals, Saracens, Slavs and sundry pirates struck here and there making chaos out of order.

The medieval period saw a succession of Venetian families controlling the islands, building walls, forts and the *kastros* or fortified hearts of settlements. Venice introduced a new splendour to the Greek islands and much of the appearance that the towns and villages possess today.

Turkish rule through the seventeenth and eighteenth centuries was by remote control rather than by massive military presence. There was no large building programme and little tangible evidence has been left of their occupation.

Turkish control may not have been a yoke that was difficult to bear but it was certainly unacceptable. The War of Independence brought to the fore heroes and heroines among the islanders such as Manto Mavrogenis. Their contribution to the history of Greece is amply recorded and remembered in the Cyclades today.

Chronological events

6000 BC Cyclades believed to have been first settled by Carians from Asia Minor and also by the Phoenicians.

4000 BC Neolithic settlements known at Mavrospilian in North Mykonos and Saliagos, Antiparos.

2800 BC Bronze Age Cycladic Civilisation developed alongside its Cretan Minoan counterpart until 1450 BC. Early sites at Naxos, Apiranthos and Sangri on Naxos and at Mt Kynthos on Delos producing curious faceless idols and marble utensils.

1600 BC Mycenaean culture from the Peloponnese present in Naxos town and on the site of the Sanctuary of Apollo in Delos.

1200 BC Pre-Classical and Classical Periods. Ionians settled in Naxos and Paros. Joined by Arcadian immigrants who extended their agriculture to Antiparos and the marble trade to Phoenicia. Naxians developed the Sanctuary of Apollo on Delos in its golden age while Demeter was worshipped in the temple at Paroikia.

708 BC Paros established a colony at Thassos in the north Aegean.

655 BC Naxians conquered Paros.

550 BC Polycrates of Samos conquered the Cyclades but Athenian rise to power led to interest in Delos.

540 BC First purification of Delos with transfer of graves to Reneia by Peisistratus of Athens.

500 BC Persian Wars. Paros sided with Persia and became a naval base.

490 BC Persians sacked Naxos while the Delians fled to Tinos. Persians then turned back at the Naval battle of Marathon.

480 BC Persians under Xerxes were defeated at the Battle of Salamis.

478 BC Delos chosen as the centre of the Delian League established to forestall future invasions.

466 BC Naxos besieged by Athenians.

426 BC Second purification of Delos by Nicias. No births or deaths permitted on the island.

431 BC Peloponnesian War. Naxos under the control of Sparta.

422 BC Athenians drove out the Delians.

404 BC Defeat of the Athenians and temporary dissolution of the Delian League.

394 BC League re-established with Athenians as masters of the Sanctuary.

375 BC Sparta defeated. Naxos again under the control of the Athenians.

338 BC Paros, Naxos and Delos under the Macedonians. Fortifications and towers of Naxos constructed.

314 BC Island League of Ptolemy I of Egypt.

166 BC Romans defeated the Macedonians bringing Cyclades under Roman control and leading to great development and prosperity on Delos.

88 BC Destruction of Delos by Mithridates, King of Pontus, in conflict with Rome.

69 BC Destruction of Delos by pirates of Athenodorus, allies of Mithridates.

60 AD Delos abandoned.

267 AD Paros pillaged by the Goths.

326 AD Byzantine Period begins. Christian development of churches and monasteries.

350 AD Naxos sacked by the Goths.

466 AD Naxos devastated by the Vandals.

769 AD Naxos sacked by Slavs.

821 AD Naxos sacked by Saracens.

1207 AD Rule by Venetian Ghizi family on Delos and Mykonos.

1210 AD Establishment of Duchy of Naxos under Marco Sanoudo and then by Sanoudo family until 1389. Aegean control from Naxos kastro and construction of castles at Apiranthos and Sangri. Sanoudo hierarchy followed by Somaripes and Crispi families.

1564 AD Turkish occupation

1644 AD Turko-Venetian War leading to the destruction of Paros and to the use of Naoussa as a pirate centre.

1770 AD Turko-Russian War in which Paros became a base for the Russian fleet and Russian sailors visited the cave of Antiparos.

1821 AD War of Independence (to 1827)

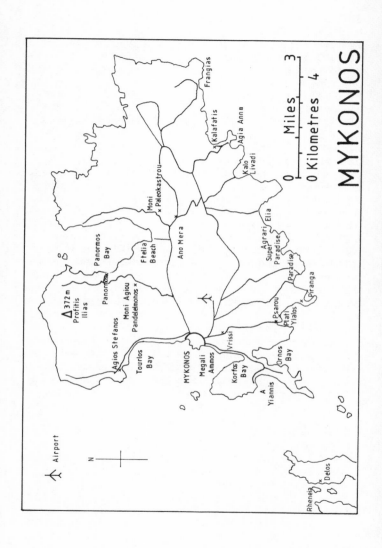

EIGHT

Mykonos

There is no place quite like Mykonos. It is an irresistible mecca for the trendy and sophisticated of western Europe and yet, at the same time, it retains the magical Cycladic qualities which set this island group apart from all others.

It would be a mistake to assume that Mykonos is a typical Greek island or that its people and its economy are similar to those of others in the Aegean. It is not a centre for fishing nor is it an agricultural community of any significance. Traditional Greek life and values are secondary to the needs of the foreigner and the lure of money: Mykonos is almost entirely devoted to the tourist. But it is not another miniature Cote d'Azur or Costa del Sol. There are no palaces of glass or concrete and the skyline is not ruptured by soaring blocks of masonry. Indeed, one of its characteristics is the profusion of chapels throughout the island — it is said that there are 365, though no one troubles to confirm or deny this suggestion. However many there are, all are delightful, ranging in form and size enormously, from the smallest chapel of Our Lady of Gatis (literally Our Lady of the Cats), which can cope with one devotee at a time, to the busy cathedral near to the Alefkandra shoreline.

Mykonos was a lure to the discerning traveller in the 1950s, with the appearance of Sophia Loren in *Boy on a Dolphin,* and the pace of tourism has hastened since then. Nevertheless, because it all began in early post-war years and the initial progress was slow, care was taken not to destroy the unique character of the town. No doubt the Mykonians were proud of their heritage and also did their utmost to preserve it. Mykonos town and island cannot be dismissed as just another holiday resort. Its size and limited facilities, as well as national tourist policy, prevent complete inundation by a summer flood of visitors. It may be crowded in places and at times but part of the enjoyment of Mykonos lies in the people who are drawn to it. Even the most ardent Hellenophile must find something unchanging and compelling on Mykonos.

Greece has managed to remain relatively cheap by European standards as the value of the drachma has declined but reasonable prices in other parts of Greece are not matched by those in Mykonos. Costs should not be a deterrent to visitors. Mykonos caters for an enormous range of visitors from students without obvious means of support to wealthy Americans who briefly leave the security of their cruise ships. There are prices for all, though a night's entertainment could prove expensive in the bars and discos for those that have developed a thirst.

Historical background

One surprising feature is the relative lack of a historical record and the artifacts which go with it. Considering the proximity of Mykonos to Delos, Naxos and Paros, it appears as an archaeological backwater. It was named after Mykonos, son of Anios, and was settled from Ionia by the descendents of King Codros of Attica. Its early inhabitants gained a reputation as spongers on society: 'Mykonian neighbours' were synonymous with a drain on resources.

The Mykonians backed the losers by supporting the Persians in the great sea battle of Salamis and duly became members of the Athenian Alliance. Culture brought some slender rewards and Mykonos issued its own coinage between the fourth and first centuries BC. The small bronze coins featured the bearded head of Dionyssos wreathed in ivy leaves on the obverse, and corn and grapes on the reverse below the abbreviation *MYKO*. Even so, Delos, Naxos and Paros had a silver coinage in keeping with their greater prosperity at that time.

Few other tangible remains have been found of pre-Roman society. Certainly the most important was the discovery near Mykonos town in 1963 of a large burial amphora dating back to the seventh century BC. It has a broad flat lip, ornately decorated and pierced handles, and a superb broad pictorial collar. The latter depicts a strutting Trojan horse, with faces peering out of trap doors at troops with crested helmets, spears and shields.

Perhaps one reason for the obscurity of Mykonos is the lack of a systematic archaeological survey. Even the location of classical settlements is shrouded in doubt though there might well have been one in the vicinity of Mykonos town. It may be that, in keeping

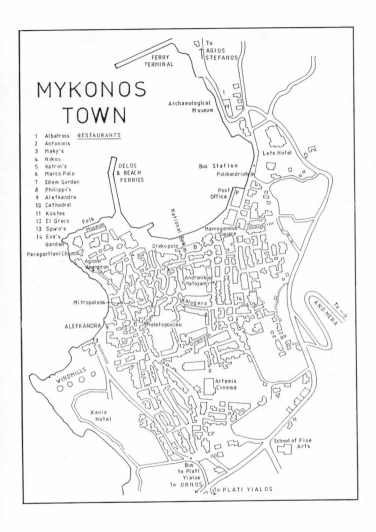

MYKONOS TOWN

RESTAURANTS

1 Albatross
2 Antoninis
3 Maky's
4 Nikos
5 Katrin's
6 Marco Polo
7 Edem Garden
8 Philippi's
9 Alefkandra
10 Cathedral
11 Kostas
12 El Greco
13 Spiro's
14 Eva's Garden

To AGIOS STEFANOS

FERRY TERMINAL

Archaeological Museum

DELOS & BEACH FERRIES

Leto Hotel

Bus Station
Polikandrioti

Post Office

Folk Museum

Paraportiani Church

Agion Anargiron

National Bank

Drakopolo

Mavrogenous Square

Androniku Matoyanni

Mitropoleos

Kalogera

To ANO MERA

ALEFKANDRA

Meletopoulou

Enameon

WINDMILLS

Artemis Cinema

Xenia Hotel

School of Fine Arts

Bus to Plati Yialos
To ORNOS

To PLATI YIALOS

with modern Greek island settlements, there were two parts to each town: a hilltop defensive *chora,* and a lower accessible port or valley site. A number of local hills around Mykonos proffer possible locations — such as Agios Georgios to the north, Marathi to the northeast, Mt Kounoupas to the east and Drafaki to the southeast; but there is no bait to attract the diggers.

Mykonos had periods of rule by Macedonians, Egyptians, Rhodians and Romans. Eventually it came under the control of a Venetian family, the Ghizis, in the thirteenth and fourteenth centuries and then by the Venetian Republic in 1390 though little remains to record their presence. In 1718 the Venetians ceded the island to the Turks, who remained until the War of Independence between 1821 and 1827. It was then that the Mavrogenis family were prominent in the struggle, as they were in Paros. Their names are recorded in the street plan, as they are in Paroikia.

Mykonos town

As with other islands in the Cyclades, urban interest does not lie in large impressive buildings or in reconstructed archaeological remains. This does not mean that the town is modern. The cottages of fishermen have formed the nucleus which has been maintained and refurbished constantly to create the town of today. The uses of many buildings have changed and a legion of additions have been made in the same mould but without the symmetry and plan of modern developments. It is the nature of its growth that appeals so much: like a coral adding to its branches, Mykonos has spread its brilliant white net in an infinite variety of ways to achieve the same harmonious effect. Beauty is present in a myriad of details and in the composite whole.

The harbour area
The harbour of Mykonos is largely protected by the wings of its two stone jetties. The northern one, away from the town centre, is larger and accommodates the main ferries which arrive daily. It is also used by the ever-increasing flow of cruise vessels which unload their cargo of tourists for a brief glimpse of its charms and an opportunity to disgorge some of their considerable wealth into the Greek economy. The smaller southern jetty is lined with motor vessels and caiques plying to Delos and the beaches. A tiny stone pier at its base is lined with still smaller open boats and crowned by a small white chapel with a low blue dome. It seems to have

no name but since it is located on the harbour it is very likely to be yet another Agios Nikolaos, as he is the patron saint of seafarers. Many of the smaller chapels were constructed by sailors grateful for surviving accidents at sea.

The Archaeological Museum is at the northern end of the bay. Unfortunately, in most countries regional museums tend to play a very poor second fiddle to the national collections to where, not surprisingly, the best artifacts gravitate. (Delos is certainly in this category.) But little has been found on Mykonos to attract national attention and it does possess its most valued treasure, the great amphora with the wooden horse relief. Many of its other exhibits have been derived from the excavation of the cemeteries on Reneia, the deserted island next to Delos.

Towards the centre of the harbour there is a small patch of sand by the Polikandrioti waterfront. This is not the most salubrious or magnetic of Mykonian beaches, except to the island drifters fresh off a late ferry and without time to organise other accommodation. The road alongside the beach is the terminus for buses to Ano Mera and to some of the beaches on the south side of the island. It is also close to other facilities, for the building block protruding out into the bay at the end of the beach contains a ticket agency, the Olympic Airways office, the Post Office and a pharmacist. The serried ranks of sleeping bags on the sand have secured for this desirable site with transport laid on the nickname of the 'Mykonos Hilton'.

Polikandrioti passes the elegant, beautiful and expensive wares on sale in Lalaounis jewellery store opposite the equally splendid fashion shop of Galatis and then enters the square of Manto Mavrogenis. A small bust in the square celebrates heroine Manto's part in repelling invaders during the War of Independence. Today, the square is a bustling place with snack bars, the Seagull 'pub' Antoninis taverna, tourist shops, the Piano Bar, a doctor's and, most important, the terminus for the island's taxi service. This augments the local bus and boat services and gives access to beaches out of their range.

In the middle of the waterfront next to the National Bank is the church of Agios Nikolaos and nearby, one street behind the harbour, is Agia Kyriaki, which contains some of the finest ikons on the island.

The old town

The tip of the promontory of Paraportiani is the site of the *kastro*, the defensive fort of Mykonos. It is the oldest part of the town,

55

Balcony gardens in Mykonos.

a labyrinth of narrow twisting ways, constructed without rhyme or reason except that its complexity helps to defeat the penetrating wind. The maze stretches from the head of the bay at Alefkandra, includes the nearby Metropolis or Cathedral, and follows the line of the winding Meletopoulou and Agiou Gerasimou to the harbour shore near Agia Kyriaki. It is crowded with chapels and curves, steps and cul-de-sacs, bars and restaurants.

Outside the packed pathways of the little peninsula, the expanded Mykonos takes on the faintest semblance of order. It is not a neat grid layout but there is some parallelism in the narrow streets. On the western side, Agion Anargiron leads into the Mitropoleos which passes the Cathedral and opens out into Agias Paraskevi and Agiou Efthimiou. To the east a series of sub-parallel streets leads inland from the square of Manto Mavrogenis beside the harbour. These include Agias Annis, Mavrogeni, Zouganeli and the flourishing Andronikou-Matoyanni. Although there is some system to this pattern, it is not always obvious on the ground and getting lost is no trouble at all especially as the land rises to the east. Steep slopes and steps climb to the ring road of Agiou Ioannou around the town and then on to the main island village of Ano Mera.

The busy cathedral of Mykonos, behind the Alefkandra shoreline and next door to the Catholic Church, is surmounted by a slender little tower with a balustrade around its tiny red dome and bears a trace of its ancient origins in the form of the symbol of the Venetian Ghizis over the doorway.

Undoubtedly the finest place of worship, at least from the outside, is the Paraportiani church. In many ways it is almost as symbolic of Mykonos as its windmills. The Paraportiani is really a complex of small chapels standing on the headland at the southern end of the harbour beyond the Delos jetty. It can't be its snowy whiteness that attracts, as most Mykonian buildings are similarly washed. Its charm lies in the way that it has grown without symmetry or pattern. Projecting buttress walls, bevelled and inclined, rise from tiny barrel vaults to the little white dome and even smaller bell arch. Deliberate and considered design could not have produced such a pleasing effect. Paraportiani is the icing on the Mykonian cake.

The Alefkandra district

South-west of the headland on which stands the Paraportiani Church is a second bay but the shoreline is largely inaccessible with buildings to the water's edge. It is possible to walk along a very short stretch beside the restaurants but it is open and exposed to north winds and waves. Adjacent is the Alefkandra district, one of the most attractive sections of town.

Both the north and south sides of this bay are distinctive and different from the rest of the Mykonos townscape. The southern side of the bay is backed by a rather scruffy slope below a level platform on which stands the remains of the five windmills known as **Kato Myli** or Lower Mills. (This distinguishes them from the two **Ano Myli** or Upper Mills near the ring road east of the town.) Three of the mills retain conical roofs and the twelve arms of the vanes. One of them is maintained in a working state, propelled by the traditional triangular sails, and it is possible to climb its wooden stairs to see and hear the groaning timbers as the wheels revolve. When, and if, all five are brought to working order, the Kato Myli will be a spectacular sight. They are well placed to receive the full power of the prevalent north winds.

The mills face the waterfront of Little Venice across the bay. The waves break directly on to the foundations of the houses. Pillars and brackets support wooden balconies projecting over the sea. The site is not only pleasing to the eye, it is regarded by the Mykonian lads as a profitable fishing ground. These houses are now largely utilised as bars and galleries whose entrances open out on to Agion Anargiron which runs parallel to the shore.

The changing moods of the town

Mavrogenis Square opens on to the waterfront mecca of the harbour. Small caiques are moored offshore and open boats line the sea wall but the mood changes with the time of day. In the morning there is commercial activity. Fishermen may be sitting on the stone flags repairing vast yellow nets with red floats while puffing away at the obligatory cigarette. In the heat of the day the town is relatively quiet. The hordes have departed for the beaches and only late arrivals and those who have had a long night before are surfacing at this stage. For some, of course, the night is what it is all about; the day is for relaxation in the shade, for drifting into the cafés and bars on the front or pottering among the *periptero* or kiosks for post cards and maps.

The merit of a Mykonian afternoon is that the Greek population see it as a natural siesta. Shipping offices, banks, the post office, the taxi service and many shops and restaurants close down. West Europeans are almost all on the south coast beaches. It is very pleasant and easy to while away the time but this is also one of the best times for the enthusiastic photographer to get to grips with the task of capturing all aspects of Mykonos. The town is pristine white, quiet and unpopulated. Nobody is walking unexpectedly into shot and it is the time to look at the narrow ways behind the waterfront. People are attracted by a variety of features and there are plenty to examine closely and fill the camera lens.

Mykonos is spotless. The whitewash is touched up on the slightest pretext and the reticule of cement between the rough-shaped flagstones receives daily whitening treatment to maintain its crazed pattern. Balustrades on external steps and wooden balconies are glossed in brown, red and blue to contrast with the white background. Heavy wooden doors and tiny windows, steps and shutters all offer potential subjects. The chapels have features in common but all are unique. They have not been designed by artists but everything about them is artistic. Their lines, their domes and their campaniles are made for the lens. Perhaps most enticing is the casual arrangement of plants in this setting. Trailing plants drip down from the window ledges while checkered dark green cylindropuntia cacti tower upwards. Branching spiny cereus peep exotically above the balconies and the ever present fine-leaved basil adorns doorsteps and windows.

Almost as typical of Mykonos as its architecture and decor in recent years has been Petros the Pelican. This singular bird (or, more precisely, birds) has been strutting around the town for more than a decade. The original Petros, having settled in Mykonos, was readily adopted by the local population and became as familiar as the Paraportiani to both Greeks and visitors. Eventually Petros took off and landed on a nearby island where the people welcomed the potential money spinner to the chagrin of the Mykonians. Irritation turned to litigation as Mykonos claimed its errant bird. The law recognised the Mykonian claim and Petros duly returned to stalk the waterfront by day and the Pelican restaurant by night, a surprisingly tolerant attraction to countless visitors.

Unfortunately even legends are lost in the mists of time and Petros was mortal. The pelican faded away to be replaced by another. It seemed such a good idea that more than one has made its appearance on the streets and, just to prove that pelicans have not got a monopoly of interest or charm, sundry other birds have appeared, most recently a hawk.

Mykonos town is a spectacular place by day. Even the most carping critic would be hard pressed to find fault with its appearance. Disapproval of its loss of Greekness may be valid but not with a townscape that has grown slowly and been moulded and nurtured by Greeks.

Mykonos by night is another world. Visitors are happy to be

59

in other parts of the island by day but by night the beaches are relatively quiet and dark. Most Greek island ports feature a nightly parade of visitors along the waterfront, back and forth to take in the lights and see the crowd. This is primarily a Greek phenomenon though Mykonos town is not, today, a resort for Greeks. The west European tourist population is much greater than the 4000 residents of the island. The tastes and needs of this seasonal population determine the use and form of the town by night.

By day Mykonos is brilliant white and silent but at night it glows gold and seethes with people. The quiet ways are transformed. The shops are open and stacked with leather ware, clothes, jewellery, cards and books. Gold and silversmiths display their creations and the skill of the clothing designers is matched only by their prices. Among the more interesting corners are those enclosures which in Britain would be rather down at heel second hand scrap yards. Here, in the uneven glimmer of artificial light, they become intriguing Aladdin's caves of quaint bric-a-brac (though the contents are not what they were a few years ago). To some the most interesting places are the shops of the weavers with their looms and heavy fabrics. Among these, Venizoulas on Enoplon Dinameon near to El Greco is fascinating, an ancient little place with hundreds of wool skeins hanging from the ceiling in a colourful array.

There is an almost unlimited choice of restaurants for the visitor. All are interesting but most cater for the cosmopolitan crowds of the island. Greek food may be served but steaks and chops cooked in a variety of west European styles, king prawns and curries figure prominently. Many of the restaurants are set attractively in gardens and other overlap on to the narrow streets, an equally pleasant prospect.

Mykonian night life has a reputation, well-deserved, for being exotic. For long it has been a summer mecca for the gay community but, rather than being a deterrent to other tourists, this has proved to be an additional interest. The dress flair and free attitude appealed to students and also to well-heeled trendies from European capitals. The more people that were attracted, the greater was the drawing power of Mykonos. A dazzling array of clothes, increasingly daring, on a summer population of beautiful people and on one of the most attractive islands in the Mediterranean made Mykonos a magnet. In response, the Greek population display incredible tolerance to the whims of the tourists even at times when the national attitude is very much against liberality. No other island has been prepared to take quite the same stand of live and let live.

Of course, Greeks are also notable business people and no doubt

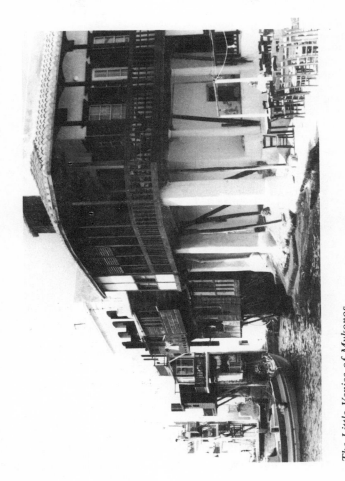

The Little Venice of Mykonos.

61

saw the commercial possibilities of the situation at an early stage. They catered for the requirements of the visitors with a host of bars and discos set out in a variety of decors. The settings were ready for outlandish and bizarre entertainment and a nightlife as appealing to many as the landscape during the day.

Mykonos is memorable and full of interest but is not, perhaps, an ideal centre for those with less than a liberal outlook.

Outside the town the island of Mykonos is rocky, bare and almost without villages. Only Ano Mera in the centre gathers together a nucleus of houses of any antiquity. On the coast there are no fishing communities but there are some of the very finest beaches in Greece. A sparse scatter of isolated farm cottages is spread over the interior in the normal pattern of other Cycladic islands.

There are two faces to the island. The northern one, open to the *meltemi,* is rocky and wave-lashed for much of the time, the coast neglected but beautiful. The wind is onshore and intolerable; sand blasting is for cleaning and not skin removal and so the crowds head to the south. Here they find a series of sheltered bays of white sand opening into smooth blue waters, an unfailing and dependable attraction.

Ornos, Psarou and Plati Yialos

The section of the coast which has been utilised for the longest period of time, not surprisingly, is that which is nearest to Mykonos town. The beaches around the town, the 'Mykonos Hilton' and Megali Ammos, are literally only last resorts, but to the south there is a group of beaches at Ornos, Psarou and Plati Yialos which are the most developed on the island. To a large degree these were created to cater for Greek holidaymakers from the mainland and they still do. These are consequently regarded as 'family' beaches and not too liberated or western in their outlook.

The peninsula forming the southwestern corner of the island terminates in Akrotiri Alogomandra. On its western side is the small beach at **Aghi Yiannis** below a little chapel of the same name while on the eastern side is the deep-set **Ornos Bay,** separated by a narrow, low isthmus from the north-facing Korfos Bay. Ornos is served by a bus from Mykonos and has hotels, tavernas and beach bars away from which most Greek holiday-makers do not stray. These naturally provide traditional Greek food but, in recent years, the new apartments at Costa Ilios have endeavoured to tempt wider interest.

A second bus service from Mykonos leads south to the beaches of Psarou and Plati Yialos. This departs every quarter of an hour in the morning and climbs over the hill to the south coast. The bus takes ten minutes to reach Psarou and another two or three to get down to Plati Yialos. The buses are always crowded in summer so the alternative is to walk, though this takes about threequarters of an hour. A second alternative is to catch a bus in the opposite direction to the terminal (at the southern end of the town beyond the Xenia Hotel) where you have a better chance of boarding the bus you want. One of the reasons for the popularity of this service is that Plati Yialos is itself a terminus for caiques plying to the other south coast beaches which receive the daily migration of sunworshippers.

Half a mile before the bus descends to its terminus at Plati Yialos is the stop for **Psarou.** Above it is the hilltop location of Lino, one of the possible sites of early Mykonos. White pensions beside the road look down the steep slope to the beach, a 150-metre strip of white sand slipping into weed-free turquoise water. The bay is enclosed by bare hillsides with granite bulging through the sparse vegetation. At the base a swaying sward of green canes behind a low stone wall creates a lush and tropical aura. At each end, tavernas serving good food peep through the greenery at their conical sun shades planted in the beach. Worth a closer look are the chapels near the sea, one at the western end of the bay and one on the tip of the headland separating Psarou from Plati Yialos. The one by the beach is a modern but beautiful vault with a graceful tracery of decorative arches. The rocks on which the headland chapel stands are granites crowded with large feldspar crystals streamed out by the flow of the originally molten rock and filtered into a crystalline log jam, striking even to inexpert eyes. For those not seeking too exotic a beach life, Psarou is a pleasant place.

Plati Yialos means wide shore, though this is perhaps an overstatement. Having been developed over a long period, it has several hotels as well as beach bars and tavernas, wind surfing and water skiing, coloured parasols and crowds. The beach is sandy but lacks the greenery of Psarou. The hillside is more liberally coated with apartments but, for many visitors, its attraction lies in its access to the beaches beyond.

By following the length of Plati Yialos beach one is led into a dusty track crossing the headland to the south. There is a low rocky shore to the right and a few flat fields over the stone wall to the left. The fields are protected from the open sea by a line of tall

63

canes leaning in the wind and by a tiny red-roofed chapel overlooking Plati Yialos bay. At the end of this shore a scimitar-shaped headland, **Akrotiri Drapanos,** projects into the sea. A low dome of bouldery granite rises from its blade and this is tenuously attached to the mainland by an isthmus of white sand with small tussocks of spiky growth. There is a beautiful strand of white sand on the eastern, **Piranga Bay,** side of the peninsula. The waters are translucent aquamarine painted more darkly where swathes of weed cling to the sandy floor. A cluster of granite slabs rises centrally through the waters to entice sunbathers away from the beach. The charms of Piranga are not lost. Coloured tents are pegged to the sand and two beachside tavernas serve the needs of the tanned denizens.

A gritty decaying granite forms the eastern side of the bay and it is home to red and mottled starfish as well as a host of urchins including some with delicate white tips to the violet spines. In places pale veins zig-zag through the rock where feldspar and quartz minerals were injected into a still plastic and moving molten granite. The rock forms a low platform terminating in a point where steep cliffs plunge into dark waters. Little tracks meander across this level into the next bay which is known as **Paradise.**

Paradise and Super Paradise

It is not too difficult to hike to Paradise but undoubtedly it is best found at the end of a caique journey. This may depart from Mykonos town and take the long route around Akrotiri Alogomandra or the shorter loop round from Plati Yialos. **Paradise Beach** nestles in at the base of the steep rocks of Akrotiri Kalamoro in a stony encircling bowl. Sparse tufts of vegetation are dispersed amid the boulders of this hot amphitheatre but the ubiquitous green cane behind the beach alleviates the barren prospect as do the two tavernas which serve its summer population. Around the well-known Freddie's Taverna is a tightly packed camp site but its discomforts are obviously outweighed by the ambience of Paradise. The taverna is a place of plastic tablecloths beneath cane awnings but most visitors like the food and the boisterous activities of the evening. Some proclaim that it is 'not what it was' but it is probably what it has been for many years, a beach of white sand and blue sea on which all inhibitions are shed.

Paradise is not just a topless beach: clothes of any description may be the exception rather than the rule. Its white hot sands are crowded with perfect unbroken tans and not a scruple in sight. However, one little blemish in this natural paradise has appeared in recent years in the form of Arab voyeurs clad from head to toe in traditional white robes.

The next port of call for caiques is around Akrotiri Kalamoro and in Karkinagri Bay. It rejoices in the name of Super Paradise and, for some, this might be true. Huge rectilinear boulders, rounded by the sun's flaking heat, bolster the flanks of the 200-metre strand set, like Paradise, in a steep sided grey bowl with no easy access except from the sea. The caiques make a very brief call to unload their cargo of devotees, most of whom are gay. Those not sharing their enthusiasm for the same sex may feel a little out of place amid those clustered in friendly conclaves along the beach, though it is at least as attractive a place as the others. However, in recent years, the tendency has been for the population to divide, the west being gay and the east otherwise.

Agrari and Elia

The motor vessels chug along close to the pale, jointed cliffs before swinging into the wide bay of Elia. Here, they make the two most distant calls on the service. This enormous arc of coast is also known as Hell, though this may simply be a mispronunciation: it is hardly hell! Some think it is Heaven. On the other hand, *elia* means olive but the site is distinctly lacking in these at the present time even if they grew here in the past.

Elia's expanse is bisected by a prong of scrub-covered rock pushing through the sand into the sparkling waters. This produces two magnificent beaches and the caique first pulls into the western half known as **Agrari.** The prow grinds into the steeply dipping sand and passengers alight by jumping off the bow ladder into the splashing surf. An elegant descent is not possible.

Until a few years ago the western beach was a virtual refuge of solitude, a broad and dazzling strand encased in tawny tufted slopes and backed by a dark green strip where a winter stream trickled down into the bay. Few bothered to trek far from the Elia terminal to cross these virginal sands. It was worth scaling the hill on its western side to gaze down on the broad sweep of both beaches and on the crenulate pattern left by the advancing and retreating waves. Such a gem could not remain undiscovered and it is now the popular Agrari Beach.

Agrari, today, suffers a little from its more open aspect inland.

Slopes are more gentle and less rocky and it is susceptible to northerly winds. Where the low green belt lay there now nestles the beach taverna, more verdant still in its swathe of swaying cane and having, according to some, the cleanest toilets on the island. The broad beach, being open to the the gusting wind, has been lined with fences of short dried cane to protect the basting bodies from the erosive blast. Nevertheless, it lacks the people packed on to Psarou and Paradise and is justly liked by many.

The rock divide that separates Agrari from Elia is laced by low stone walls which divide the landscape into impossible and uneconomic parcels of land. A closely jointed little arch of cream and ochre coloured granite caps the outcrops and picks up a whisper of wind to ameliorate the heat when the meltemi drops. Little embayments of sand interdigitate the rocks and the view is striking in all directions.

Elia is the most distant call of the ferries and, usually, two or three boats bob up and down in the gentle waves which lap its shore, adding a splash of colour to the superb beach. The view from imposing Kavos Elias at the end of the beach reveals that the majority of visitors cluster close to the caiques where the sands are at their narrowest and crossed by mooring ropes. It is always surprising that people are so gregarious in these circumstances. However, this spot is favoured by Italians and that might account for a lot.

The beach is broad as well as long and supports two restaurants, the Elia Beach and Matheos. Both offer respite in the heat of the day, a good range of dishes and a cold drink to instil fortitude for the next round of tanning. A large proportion of the visitors to Elia are topless and many regard costumes as an unnecessary encumbrance but in such a beautiful setting it all seems very natural.

Kalo Livadi

At the eastern end of Elia a dirt track cuts across a small spur, descends to a bouldery beach and then climbs past a white cottage on the flank of Kavos Elias. A slender thicket of fresh-looking bullrushes surprisingly decorates the track side at one point, thriving on the outflow of water from the cottage. The path has been carved recently out of the scrub and boulders of the steep slope and then abandoned, going nowhere. Rains have gullied its tawny soils down to the bare rock, rendering it unusable by even fourwheel-drive vehicles. The climb on foot is not difficult and the top reveals not only the sweep of Elia Bay, looking back, but also the deep bay of Kalo Livadi and, more distant, Kalafatis beyond.

Kalo Livadi, beautiful meadow, lies beyond Kavos Elias. In keeping with its distance from the town, it is less used. It is also less accessible as the caiques do not visit it. The normal procedure to reach it is to hire a taxi from Manto Mavrogenis Square and to arrange for a return pick up at an appointed hour. The Mykonian taxi drivers are normally very reliable. The route follows the tarmac to Ano Mera on the central plateau of Mykonos then descends through a V-shaped notch in the granite to one of the flat cultivable pieces of the island, the meadow of its name. This is neatly tilled, with dry stone walls outlining the rectilinear plots. A handful of trees are scattered about the little plain and a few isolated lines of cane have been planted to frustrate the rush of wind through the valley. There are white cottages dotted about the farmland to create a little rural paradise in the tourist-oriented world of Mykonos.

At the mouth of the valley lies the beach of Kalo Livadi, scalloped by the lapping waves and one of the finest on the island. Gentle buff slopes on its flanks and the little valley behind unfortunately open it to the wind whistling in from the north. At the eastern end of the beach is its single restaurant, though for long there were no services there. At the other end, raised a little above the sand, is a barrel-vaulted chapel with a glowing red roof and a stepped gable leading up to the tiny belfry. As is typical of Greece, it is maintained in pristine condition.

Beyond the chapel, cliffs loom steeply over the sand and provide a shelter against the wind and the best place to be on a breezy day. Large boulders rest on the sand and produce the very limited shade available. The grey granite boulders repay inspection by those seeking respite from the long business of cooking themselves on the beach. The rock has been attacked by waves and salt spray so that the finer grained minerals of feldspar, quartz and mica have gradually been eaten away. This has left the large rectangular crystals of white orthoclase feldspar projecting like tubercles on a crocodile's back. Where the crystals have been broken they demonstrate their simple twin structure by one half shining glassily while the other is dull.

Agia Anna Bay and Kalafatis

A dirt road skirts the east of Kalo Livadi Bay passing miniature coves cased in granite walls. It heads for the gaunt, hollow-eyed frame of a disused mine on the cape of Skala Fortoseos. A spidery metal arm, intended for offloading minerals, pokes into the bay, a skeleton in every sense of the word. Mining has never been of paramount importance in the Greek islands and even more successful operations, such as the emery working in Naxos, have become defunct. At Skala Fortoseos baryte is present where the roof of the granite has baked overlying rocks into a dark hornfels, but fickle demand and fluctuating price have bedevilled marginal activities already beset by escalating costs.

Above the mine, the headland is partitioned by dry stone walls which enclose an unexpected number of sheep, cows and even pigs. The highest point looks down to the perfect little arc of white sand in **Agia Anna Bay.** Twin rocky points almost seal the circular and beautiful anchorage for a handful of yachts. A small taverna serves the tiny community on one side and the shells of a few incomplete bungalows herald changes in the future.

The eastern cape of the bay is attached by a narrow isthmus of white sand tying it to the long sweep of **Kalafatis** beach. Yellow gentle slopes drop down to Kalafatis from the west and steeper ones from the east. Other bays of the south coast have tavernas which seem to merge with the landscape without really spoiling it. Most are single-storey and are set in thickets of canes but at Kalafatis there is a complex of buildings at the northern end of the beach belonging to the Aphroditi Hotel. This includes bungalows and larger dwellings, a beachside taverna and a disco. Gardens have been laid out as well as a fringe of green shade trees beside the sand and around the restaurant. Kalafatis is a fine beach and facilities, no doubt, please many but it is not in the pattern which makes Mykonos such an attraction. As it is out on a limb away from the magnet of the town, there is a bus service provided by both the transport authority and by the hotel itself.

The north coast beaches

The most easterly parts of Mykonos are among the highest. The peak is named, traditionally, Profitis Ilias and reaches 341 metres. Less traditionally, its summit is dominated not by a white chapel but a vast radar dome and a military presence with the usual ban on photography. There are beaches for isolationists in inaccessible positions at **Lia** and **Frangias** to the east and at **Fokos** and **Kakopati** to the north.

Most of the north coast is a trackless waste in response to its exposure to the cold blasts of winter and to the persistent raking by the *meltemi*. The coastline is bifurcated by the enormous Panormos Bay which stretches almost to the heart of the island. Small sinuous dirt tracks follow the sides of the bay. The western route reaches the entrance adjacent to the 372-metre peak of yet another Profitis Ilias but this one is made of marble metamorphosed from limestones by heat originally emitted by the granite. The same rock forms Marmaronissi, the Marble Islands, in the mouth of the bay.

There are two beaches on the bay, each served by a restaurant in season. **Panormos Beach** in the middle of the north coast is regarded by many as the very best on the island but unfortunately throughout many days the sand blast is intolerable. The other beach is at the head of the bay and is called **Ftelia.** It is backed by a treeless waste which accumulates debris drifted in the wind. It does have the merit of being close to the metalled road from Mykonos and adjacent to the central village of Ano Mera.

Ano Mera

Ano Mera, 8 km from Mykonos, is the only village outside the town. It is a small focus for the large number of rural dwellings which are dispersed across the centre of the island. The bare stony hills disguise the productivity of the area. The patches of smoothly tilled brown earth and the dense spread of neat white buildings give a more realistic picture.

The centre of Ano Mera, as in many villages, is the *plateia* or square. Here it is broad, open and set like a plateau raised on high. On one side local vegetables are sold from hand balances and on the other stands a most traditional *kafeneion*. Large eucalyptus trees provide the shade for its tables which are arranged on the square itself and on a raised platform alongside. Straw-hatted old men chat over their small cups of coffee, a picture in themselves. This is a little cell of old-fashioned Greek life holding out against change. Ano Mera's defence has been aided by its distance from the beaches and the high life of Mykonos. It still produces ouzo and *kopanisti* cheese but even here the modern world has made inroads in the form of an 'A' grade hotel with a swimming pool.

This endeavours to get the best of both worlds from its rural setting by providing bus services to Mykonos into the middle of the night and to Elia beach during the day. The process works in reverse, too, as some tour agencies organise 'traditional' evenings out from the frenetic activity of town to a taverna in Ano Mera.

Adjacent to the square and just below it is the monastery church of Panaghia Tourliani with its massive white walls and bright red dome. Brass studded doors open to reveal steps leading down into the courtyard. The church has an unexpected smooth marble facade and a tall campanile rising above the dome. In a corner opposite the west door is a marble drinking fountain carved in the form of a face and dated 1787. Its metal cup is chained to the wall, surely not a necessary precaution in a Greek village. A narrow way separates the church from the monastic cells, a quiet white rivulet shaded by eucalyptus. The external interest of the church is matched by a dark and ornate interior in keeping with its significance in the village. In fact, Ano Mera possesses a second monastery just to the north at Paleokastrou. This is a nunnery, very similar in external appearance to Tourliani, attractively set in a splash of green on a bare hillslope.

The northwest coast

The remaining development on Mykonos is concentrated on the fresh and breezy west coast to the north of the town. The most northerly amenities are at **Houlakas** where there are a couple of tavernas. A hilly headland terminating in the islet of Galatonissi separates Houlakas from the more sheltered resort of **Agios Stefanos,** one of the more rapidly growing settlements. There is a sandy beach on which topless sunbathing is permitted but not the total freedom of the south. There are several very reasonable hotels and restaurants close to the beach while apartments and rooms have sprung up on the slopes behind. A problem to visitors can be the noise of discos blasting out into the night when many would prefer to sleep. In any case dedicated dancers head for the more bizarre spots of Mykonos.

One of the advantages of the Agios Stefanos coast is that it is closely followed by a tarmac road used by a bus service from Polikandrioti. This service takes only ten minutes from town. Alternatively, it is a forty-minute walk. The road leaves the Agios Stefanos beach, tucked into the base of the headland, and then follows the wider Tourlos Bay with its line of apartments and small hotels and restaurants. The route then enters the northern spread of Mykonos town passing the main ferry jetty to reach the harbour.

Some of the Aegean Islands are extensively cutlivated while others are swathed in olives or in pines. The Cyclades are rocky, bare and dramatic islands with a most distinctive architecture. Their yellowed summer slopes under cloudless blue skies are both an image and a reality. Mykonos typifies the image more than any other island though its reality may be less than sublime.

Accommodation

Hotels on Mykonos

Class	Name	Location	Beds	Tel. (code 0289)
A	Ano Mera	Ano Mera	124	71215
A	Leto	Mykonos	48	22207
B	Andronikos	Mykonos	12	22477
B	Despotika	Mykonos	40	22009
B	Kouneni	Mykonos	36	22301
B	Les Moulins	Mykonos	26	23240
B	Rohari	Mykonos	99	23107/9
B	Vassiliou	Mykonos	24	—
B	Theoxenia	Mykonos	93	22230
B	Petasos	Mykonos	31	22608
C	Belou	Mykonos	16	22589
C	Le Village	Mykonos	24	22961
C	Manto	Mykonos	26	22330
C	Marianna	Mykonos	43	22072
C	Marios	Mykonos	20	22704
C	Mykonos	Mykonos	30	22434
C	Mykonos Beach	Mykonos	32	22572/3
C	Zannis	Mykonos	36	22481
C	Zorzis	Mykonos	20	22167
B	Konhyli	Vrissi	55	22107
C	Korali	Vrissi	54	22929
C	Magas	Vrissi	37	22577
B	Irene	Tourlos	27	22306
B	Rhenia	Tourlos	70	22300
B	Alkistis	Agios Stefanos	182	22332/3
C	Artemis	Agios Stefanos	39	22345
C	Panorama	Agios Srefanos	51	22337
C	Korfos	Korfos	42	22850
B	Ornos Beach	Ornos	40	22243
C	Anargyros	Ornos	26	22116
C	Paralos Beach	Ornos	76	22600
C	Pigal	Ornos	17	—
C	Petinos	Platis Yialos	55	22127
B	Aphroditi	Kalafatis	180	71367

Eating out

Restaurants in Mykonos town

Eating out in Mykonos can be a pleasure not only to the palate but also to the eye. Only the pocket suffers a little. Many restaurants are not traditionally Greek in character but cater for the upper end of the market by having table cloths, serviettes, candles and prices to match. These will provide enormous variety in their menus, appealing decor and a suitable setting. Others lack some of the finesse but are still eating places, much of the ambience being provided by the Greeks themselves. The location of those listed is shown on the map on page 53.

El Greco Built around the three wells of the Tria Pigadia district in the heart of Mykonos town about an equal distance from the Alefkandra shore and the harbour. A eucalyptus tree and a canvas awning provide the shade and sunflowers and corn plants the colour. The food is hot and well presented. Try the swordfish either as steaks or kebabs.

Edem Garden Located on Kalogera between Tria Pigadia and the harbour, the Edem has a pleasant enclosed garden with spectacularly large flowering cereus cacti climbing up the walls. There is attentive service and a great variety of interesting dishes on the menu. Pepper steaks are good but, for the adventurous, try the superb octopus in wine sauce or the *arni ambelougou,* filleted clove-flavoured lamb wrapped in vine leaves.

Philippi's Again in the Tria Pigadia district, Philippi's has steps leading down to a sunken garden illuminated by basket caged lights in the trees. A most attractive setting for well prepared food.

Marco Polo On the little open square of Ioannis Meletopoulou, a short distance from the cathedral. There is a white canvas awning to provide the shade and a central cluster of sunflowers. The site is not spectacular but Marco Polo is justly popular for its Greek atmosphere and food.

Katrin Just a little way behind the harbour at the intersection of Nikiou and Petros Drakopolo, Katrin's has heavy pine furniture, red cloths, elegance and French cuisine.

Eva's Garden Tucked away in a quiet white backwater at the upper end of Kalogera, this is another fine restaurant, pleasingly decorated by climbing bougainvillea and a huge *pithoi* or ornamental pot.

Alefkandra In the shade of a eucalyptus by the Alefkandra waterfront with a view to the windmills when canvas awnings are not needed to keep out the *meltemi*. It is associated with the pelican, though the bird spreads its favours around the town. The Alefkandra is noted for its lobsters, fish and suckling pig which can be seen rotating on the spit.

The Cathedral Enclosed by white church walls on the flags beside the cathedral. An extensive range of dishes is on offer but the swordfish kebabs and baby squid might be recommended. Try also the unusual fish salad.

Kostas Taverna On Mitropoleos at the entrance to Meletopoulou, a very busy corner site shaded by a eucalyptus and awnings. This is a typical Greek taverna, buzzing with activity and with reasonably priced dishes such as *paidakia* and lamb and vegetable casserole.

Spiro's Right on the water's edge below the windmills though the site shrinks before the *meltemi* waves. The evening view with the sunset, the dark outline of Tinos, illuminated cruise ships and the balconies of Little Venice cannot fail to appeal. Spiro's is noted for its lobsters and fish but try its *garides saganaki,* large prawns in spicy sauce below a cheese crust.

Albatross North of the town above the Yacht Club with a verandah and a view into the setting sun. There is smart service to accompany good steaks and the rattle of the rigging.

Antonini's Tables stretch out on to Mavrogenis Square. Antonini's is popular and reliable but can also be busy and overcrowded.

Other commendable restaurants include **Sardam, Bill's Place, Mykonos, Maky's, Nikos, Skarpa Taverna** and **Barkia Pizzeria.**

Restaurants outside town

Most restaurants outside town are at their busiest during the lunch hour. In the evening clients migrate to Mykonos though local campers may while away the long hours on site.

Plati Yialos This is the only location with a concentration of hotel and restaurant facilities. The **Petinos,** which lies at the end of the Mykonos road, has a traditional 'Greek' evening on a Saturday night with lamb roasted on the spit. The barbecue is good but the 'tradition' will not appeal to everyone.

A series of restaurant/bars stretches along the beach, each with its sun bleached deckchairs and umbrellas. These are the **Plati Yialos Hotel,** the **Agrogiali,** the **Plati Yialos Restaurant, Giorgios Taverna** and **Anna's Restaurant and Hotel.**

Island Beach restaurants Most other beaches are similarly equipped, not just with a beach bar but with one or more restaurants. Thus there are two on Psarou, three on Piranga and two on Paradise. All of these are competent but some endear themselves by virtue of one characteristic or another.

Freddie's Very popular because it is part of the camp site on Paradise Beach, supplying not only the campers but the hordes flocking in by boat each day. Standards of food are high and it is noted for its fruit salad. The waiters are prone to dance.

Agrari Beach A self-service restaurant with friendly Greeks and exceptionally clean toilets! Has cane for shade and windbreaks and caged canaries for decor.

Matheos One of the two restaurants on Elia Beach, noted for its food and service, as is the solitary **Kalo Livadi** restaurant around the headland of Kavos Elias.

Mykonos bars

To many visitors one of the most memorable features of Mykonos, at least at night, is the proliferation of bars with divers decors and larger than life clientele. Whatever the visitor seeks is there.

Thalamis An attractive place to both Mykonians and visitors beside the little chapel on the harbour. Comfortable and pleasing to both eye and ear with Greek music.

Minotaur On Mitropoleos near to the cathedral. Candle lit with solid, dark, comfortable furniture, jazz blues music and large measure cocktails.

Pierro's A gay disco seething with people between 10.00 pm and 3.00 am. The place to see and in which to be seen especially if the company is interesting and if you like large busted drag acts miming to Shirley Bassey.

The City Managed with style and elegance amid coiffeurs, kaftans and marbles. Also features drag shows.

Vengera On a corner site between Enoplon Dinameon and Andronikon Matoyanni. One of the places to visit with a colonial atmosphere, shutters and turn of the century bric-a-brac. Gay participants and staff establish a friendly ambience. The lively music has been known to induce chamois clad nymphs into a strip tease dance and police to pay a visit.

Caprice Another bar jammed tight with young set devotees of the Jacksons.

Kastro A quiet, classical music bar beside Paraportiani.

Scandinavia The in-place for young people to drink by day and night, close to the harbour.

Remezzo Overlooks the harbour from the north close to the museum. The Remezzo has a fine view, a popular disco and higher prices.

Stavro's Irish Bar Like a dark Dublin pub behind a white Cycladic arch. Stavro's is almost adjacent to Pierro's and is a mecca for Guinness and ceilidh music.

All night bars with snacks are found at the **Yacht Club** and **Pigeon Club.** Other disco bars include **Nine Muses, Rainbow, Pavlo's** and **Apollo 2000** while the **Argo, Troubadour, TK's, Anchor, Seagull** and **Piano** bars also attract many.

Vessel	Monday	Tuesday	Wednesday	Thursday	Friday	Saturday	Sunday
Panaghia Tinou	Piraeus (d.14.15)	Piraeus (d.14.15)	Piraeus (d.14.15)	Piraeus (d.14.15)	Piraeus (d.14.15)	Piraeus (d.14.15)	Piraeus (d.14.15)
Eptanisos		Tinos Andros Rafina (d.13.30)	Tinos Andros Rafina (d.13.30)		Rafina (d.23.30)	Rafina (d.23.30)	Tinos Andros Rafina (d.13.30)
Naias II	Tinos Piraeus (d.14.00)	Tinos Syros Piraeus (d.14.30)	Tinos Piraeus (d.14.00)	Tinos Syros Piraeus (d.14.30)	Tinos Piraeus (d.14.00)	Tinos Syros Piraeus (d.14.30)	Tinos Syros Piraeus (d.14.00)
Giorgios Express					Paros Ios Santorini (d.23.00)		
Nearchos			Ios Santorini Heraklion			Syros Ios Santorini Heraklion (d.13.30)	

Table 11   Ferries from Mykonos operating in most weather conditions

Vessel	Monday	Tuesday	Wednesday	Thursday	Friday	Saturday	Sunday
Skopelitis			Naxos Iraklia Schinoussa Koufonissia Amorgos (d.14.00)			Naxos Iraklia Schinoussa Koufonissia Amorgos (d.14.00)	Naxos Iraklia Schinoussa Koufonissia Amorgos (d.14.00)
Megalochari	Paros Ios Santorini (d.09.00)	Paros Ios Santorini (d.09.00)	Paros Ios Santorini (d.09.00)	Paros Ios Santorini (d.09.00)	Paros Ios Santorini (d.09.00)	Paros Ios Santorini (09.00)	Paros (d.11.00)
Ios	Paros Ios Santorini (d.16.00)	Paros Ios Santorini (d.16.00)	Paros Ios Santorini (d.16.00)	Paros Ios Santorini (d.16.00)	Paros Ios Santorini (d.16.00)	Paros Ios Santorini (d.16.00)	Paros Ios Santorini (d.16.00)

Table 12   Ferry services from Mykonos which are dependent on wind conditions

(In addition to these vessels, there are many small excursion boats which make the half-hour journey to Delos. There are also caiques, such as the *Delfini*, which first visit Delos and then deserted beaches on adjacent Rhenia for a barbecue.)

NINE

Delos

A pair of arid, barren islands lie to the southwest of Mykonos, offering an unattractive prospect to settlers past or present. These outcrops are known collectively as the Diles and comprise Delos and Renos, or Rheneia as the latter is now known. In spite of their hostile appearance, the islands were first occupied nearly 5000 years ago and Delos has had a focal place in Greek history since 1600 BC with the development of Mycenaean culture.

There are no direct major ferry services to Delos. The harbour as it stand today could not cope with large vessels. Neither is the island able to cater for residents; the small Xenia hotel has only seven beds. The principles established during its period of Athenian domination during the sixth and fifth centuries BC, in which neither births nor deaths were permitted on the island, virtually applies today. In spite of its drawbacks, Delos is as great a magnet today as it was during the prosperity of the Athenian and Roman periods. Vast numbers of tourists flock to the island to inspect its devastated ruins and marvel at the remarkable preservation of the mosaics.

The principal means of approaching the island is by the small motor ferries which ply from the small jetty at the south of Mykonos harbour in a regular stream. An alternative is to cross from Naxos. This route uses the *Daphne II,* a small but fairly speedy ship with a limited amount of deck space and a larger cabin to keep out the elements. The *Daphne II* makes its call at Delos en route to a three-hour stop in Mykonos and then returns directly to Naxos. This journey can be used simply as a means of getting from Naxos to Mykonos or it can be taken as a day excursion to Mykonos. On the latter, Delos is an appetising starter to the main course, even if this only generates an appetite for second helpings. The movements of *Daphne II* are prone to suffer from the ravages of the *meltemi* and it wisely does not venture forth when in doubt. If it operates, it heads due north out of Naxos harbour straight

79

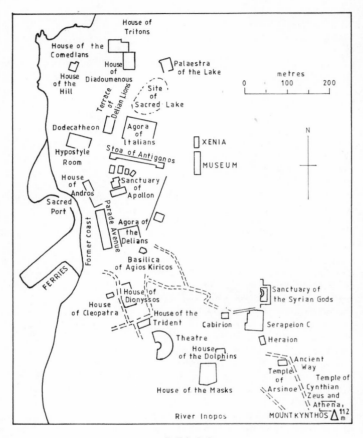

DELOS

into the wind and white horses. When the weather is good there is a possibility of an accompaniment of dolphins, first streaming alongside or in advance of the bows and then describing a series of arcs through the air at some distance from the ship.

A rough stone jetty which projects from the shores of a bay on the west coast of Delos protects the small fleet of caiques and tourist motor vessels which arrive daily. A turnstile is placed strategically at the base of this quay to ensure that all who land pay for their quota of culture. The tours from Naxos and Mykonos involve a one-and-a-half hour stop on Delos. This can be a highlight for the enthusiast but it can also be a feat of hot and thirsty endurance for those who merely want to reach Mykonos.

Background to Delos

Delos is the mythical birthplace of Apollo and Artemis though, in the case of the former, this is a claim disputed by Naxians. There are remains of habitation on Mt Kynthos, the highest point, dating back to 2000 BC but it became a cult centre and settlement in Mycenaean times after 1600 BC. Mycenaeans were followed by Ionians and the cult of Leto, Dorians and the supporters of Artemis, and by the worshippers of Apollo, notably the Athenians. They were responsible for the purification of the island. No births or deaths were permitted and all ancient graves were excavated, the contents being transferred to the adjacent island of Renos. Classical Greek architecture enhanced the rocky island with its temples, treasuries and stoa or arcades. Delos was not only a religious focus; it was established as a festival centre with the foundation of the Delian Games. These were held every four years and were inaugurated by the arrival of a state ship from Marathon, supposedly that of Theseus himself.

The decline of Athens brought brief periods of independence then occupation by the Romans and a resurgence of trade. It was a free port, commercial exchange and slave market having regular connections with Beirut, Alexandria and Tyre. Business prosperity was associated with the construction of rich merchants' houses and facilities for travellers, the remains of which are among the most attractive features of Delos.

Sadly for posterity, the Romans, too, could not maintain indefinite law and order in the Cyclades. Delos was first demolished by the forces of Mithridates and then, after reconstruction, was laid waste once more by pirates. To compound the vandalism of philistine raiders, later ages saw the use by Venetians and Turks of the whole site as one vast builders' supply yard, an almost inexhaustible store of faced stones, column blocks and statuary.

For a little over one hundred years French archaeologists have been endeavouring to make order out of the chaos in Delos. Much has been revealed but some mysteries still remain, as well as several thousand tons of disordered debris. Some aspects of the Delian scene have been removed almost without trace so there are areas which attract few tourists.

Mount Kynthos

Most people turn their feet initially to the viewpoint on the highest hill of the island, Mt Kynthos. This is a hot trek but it is only 123 metres high. There are roughly paved ancient ways to the summit so that it can be scaled even in the most unsuitable footwear. In fact it often is. A little to the right, below the path, is the Grotto of Kynthos which is believed to have been a sanctuary to the Hellenistic cult of Hercules. The view from the summit across the extensive ruins which clothe the western slopes of the island down to the rocking vessels in the harbour is most pleasant. It is never quiet or unoccupied in season as thousands of feet tread the paths to the hill top. Originally a temple to Zeus and Athena crowned this eminence but there is only fragmentary evidence of it.

The rest of the island is relatively flat and rocky with a covering of short spiny tussocks though in spring it is green and massed with flowers. It is nearly 5 km long but little over 1 km wide. Certainly it is a barren place today with its layered granite everywhere close to the surface glistening, as the sun is reflected from its flakes of muscovite mica

To the north of the harbour

Ancient Delos was built around the **Sacred Lake** and supplied by the Inopos reservoir and river but the rains of that period must have been greater than those of today. A slightly greener aspect and a solitary planted palm betray the location of the Sacred Lake which has been dry since 1925. Supposedly it was drained to remove the problem of the malarial mosquitoes but surface water is not a feature of a Delian summer. Delos blisters in the sun and the only water lies in the granite joints which provide the meagre supply

Delos lion.

of the island's few wells. A little more occupies tanks such as the arched cistern of the Theatre after the winter rains.

The renowned festival of the Delian Games took place in the northeastern corner of the island in the lee of the headland of Akrotiri Paniotis. Little remains of the stadium, the xystos or covered running track, the Hippodrome or the Gymnasium. A track leads over to this area from the side of the museum but the hot wastes deter would-be viewers. More of the palaestras are found by the northeast side of the former Sacred Lake and these are more accessible. A palaestra was a ring or arena believed to have been used for wrestling bouts.

Delos does not possess architecturally splendid temples or agora. Most buildings have been reduced to fragments though some rough walls remain relatively complete. Even the marble slabs of the Theatre have, to a large degree, been lifted and reduced to rubble and yet Delos has a unique antique quality. One reason for this is the almost total absence of modern dellings. Apart from keepers and those providing the very limited public facilities, Delos is uninhabited. The twentieth century intrudes minimally into Classical Greece.

The plan of Delos can be followed more or less as it was if only because the paved roadways have been left intact. Whereas in a city like Athens, the remaining gems of a magnificent culture are left embedded within enveloping concrete, here the whole infrastructure is present. The major buildings have gone but the ordinary houses have not. Their crumbling walls are enhanced by the thistles and grey-green rosettes of velvet leaves protruding through the cracks. They also provide a home for a multitude of lizards, large and small. Splay-toed geckoes race for cover, their dark barred backs imitating the shadowed fissures in the walls. It is not difficult to find oneself diverted from the archaeological mysteries into those of nature.

Remains that inevitably attract the interest of all lie in the centre of the site within the **Precinct of Dionyssos.** These are the incredible sculptures of two erect phalloi raised on pedestals with figurative reliefs but, sadly, beheaded in a past age. Apart from giving either an incentive or an inferiority complex to the inhabitants, this must have been a labour of as much interest to the sculptor, or sculptress, as it is to those visitors of today who can recognise what it was.

In slightly better state is the **Terrace of the Delian Lions.** This has been restored even within recent years. Originally there may have been a line up of sixteen beasts. They have undergone the usual vandalism of unappreciative ages past but have also suffered

Terrace of the Delian lions

the depredations of climatic decay. The crystalline white marble, being slowly soluble in rain water, has weathered chemically with each winter's rains so that the details of the features have gradually been erased. Limbs have been broken and some have been lost but they are not without a leg to stand on! Concrete pillars and steel rods have come to the aid of the lions. Individually one or two still present a pleasant picture and the row of five facing east to the Sacred Lake is not a disappointment.

Between the Delian Lions and the embarkation jetty lies the heart of ancient Delos, the **Apollo Sanctuary.** To be quite truthful this is a scene of total devastation and almost impossible for the ordinary visitor to envisage in its former glory. It lay immediately beside the **Sacred Port** which today is the little bay on the north side of the disembarkation jetty. Alongside the harbour is the **Stoa of Philip of Macedon,** still recognisable because of its few stunted columns parallel to the flagged **Parade Avenue.** This led to the **Propylaea** or Gateway to the Sanctuary and the adjacent **House of the Naxians** where there was originally housed a gigantic statue of Apollo, ten metres high. The huge base still stand together with a couple of large fragments of the torso. Not surprisingly, the more recognisable pieces of the left hand and foot reside with the plinth in the British Museum.

To the south of the harbour

South of the harbour on the northern slopes of Mt Kynthos there lay a residential area on either side of the Theatre. These houses were built during the second century BC when Delos was commercially at its zenith. Superficially they are not spectacular, being externally faced with rough cut grey stone. They are roofless and rather decrepit but contain a remarkable number of **mosaic floors.** While looting columns and stone blocks has been a practical proposition over centuries, it has fortunately been impossible to lift crumbling mosaic tiles. Some have broken up but many are intact and provide the most lasting memory of Delos. Houses, such as that of Cleopatra, may be named after their owners. (In this case it is an Athenian and not an Egyptian bearer of the name.) In other cases the houses are described by either their mosaic floors or their location.

On the harbour side of the Theatre are the Houses of Cleopatra, Dionyssos and the Trident. The **House of Cleopatra** lacks mosaics of note but has the headless statues of its owners sightlessly facing its interior columns. The **House of Dionyssos,** too, has a peristyle of smooth white pillars as well as a mosaic of a winged Dionyssos on the back of a tiger. Unfortunately time has not been kind to this floor and cement rendering patches the glowing tones of the tiger. The **House of the Trident** is adjacent to the Theatre. Within is one of the best collections of small mosaics. The trident in the name is set diagonally across a white marble square with a bow dancing in the middle of the haft. Other floors show a black dolphin twined around a brown anchor, an amphora set in a key pattern, and a mosaic of geometric cubes which appear solid and recessed in turn.

South of the Theatre are the Houses of the Dolphins and the Masks. In the **House of the Dolphins** paired intertwined dolphins, under the guidance of Eros, twist around a circular disc with wave and key motifs. Also in the house is the delightful little cartoon character which is the symbol of the goddess Tanit. However, the finest of all the mosaics is in the **House of the Masks** where Dionyssos, draped luxuriously in keeping with the prosperity of the heyday of Delos, rides sidesaddle on a prancing, open clawed leopard.

The **Theatre** itself nestles in a hollow at the foot of Mt Kynthos. Unfortunately, the concentric rows of regular marble slabs proved irresistible to Mykonian and other builders. The slopes of the shallow amphitheatre are littered with broken blocks through which spikes of yellow flowered verbascum rise amid a profusion of seasonal poppies. Now, little more than the first two rows of seating remain and these represent an incomplete reconstruction. The Delian Theatre is a small, pale image of the giants at Epidauros and Athens.

Delos is interesting even to the visitor whose heart is not in ancient stones, but it is dry and hot in summer and an hour and a half will be enough for most people. Those with real archaeological enthusiasm will find it inadequate to see the whole site, especially if part of the time is spent pursuing a drink: not only has Delos a barren landscape, it also possesses a near arid buffet in the facility available to the public. The solitary barman is assailed by a frenzy of tourists all urgently desiring to slake their thirst at the waterhole. He is unimpressed and inured to their pitiful cries not least because his only water supply consists of a few plastic containers of tepid fluid to top up the orange juice. Those approaching Delos from Mykonos will be able to make a second journey but for the traveller from Naxos it is not so easy.

Soon the boat swings out of the shelter of the rough jetty and into the Delos Channel alongside the rocky islet of Little Rhevmatiari. It emerges from the straits, dscribes a broad arc around Kavouronissi and heads into the clustered white cubes of Mykonos.

Accommodation

Hotel on Delos

Class	Name	Location	Beds	Tel. (code 0289)
B	Xenia	Delos	7	22259

TEN

Naxos

The raked prow of the orange-hulled ferries which ply to Paros and Naxos cut through the dark waters of the Aegean even during the more violent excesses of the northerly *meltemi*. The vessels are relatively modern, unlike some linking the islands, with twin funnels set astern bearing the company's emblem of a map of Naxos. The deep, powerful chug of the motors inspires confidence and suggests speed but the journey to Naxos takes up to eight hours from Piraeus with a stop at Paros en route.

Inevitably, the outward journey is interesting: islands appear and are lost on the horizon and passengers look forward eagerly to their destination. The decks are alive with the perpetual motion of people, the noise of Greek families and the sounds of a dozen languages. Pale, black-clad Greek women endure the commotion with stoicism and express little emotion at the sight of bikinis and exposed bronzed skins of Scandinavians and Germans. The return journey is different: the pleasures of the islands lie behind and ahead is the turmoil of Piraeus and Athens.

An alternative and regular service is available from the port of Rafina, forty-five minutes ride east of central Athens. The ugly, utilitarian, grey-hulled transporter *Atlas II* makes the trip and calls in at Syros as well as Paros on its way to Naxos, a journey of less than six hours.

Naxos town

The approach to Naxos is impressive. The island is large but compact and mountainous, with white sandy shorelines which can be seen extending along much of the western coast. First impressions of Naxos town are enchanting. Its white box-like dwellings reach from the shore up to the summit of a conical hill

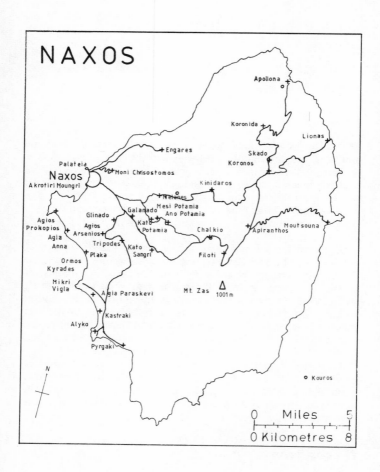

NAXOS

Apollona

Koronida

Lionas

Engares

Skado
Koronos

Palateia
Naxos + Moni Chrisostomos
Akrotiri Moungri

Kinidaros

Melanes

Mesi Potamia
Galanado Ano Potamia

Glinado

Agios
Prokopios
Kato
Potamia

Chalkio

Moutsouna

Agios
Arsenios

Apiranthos

Agia
Anna

Tripodes

Kato
Sangri

Ormos
Kyrades

Plaka

Filoti

Mikri
Vigla

Agia Paraskevi

Mt. Zas △
1001 m

Kastraki

Alyko

Pyrgaki

N

○ Kouros

0   Miles   5
0 Kilometres 8

at the edge of the green plain of Livadia. Protecting it from the north is a slender headland, tipped by the island of Palateia. This is the gateway to Naxos, surmounted by a tall, white marble arch, the former entrance to the Temple of Apollo.

First impressions may be important but Naxos rewards further investigation. To return to places long remembered may often result in disappointment but Naxos is like a good wine. Not only has it kept well but it has improved with time.

It is, of course, impossible for any place to remain unchanged. Small hotels and rooms have been developed especially on the south side of town towards St George's Bay but these have not affected either the skyline or the character of Naxos. In the same direction new tavernas and discos have gradually developed along the shoreline of the bay but surprisingly little change has resulted. The waterfront has been protected from the ravages of increased traffic by limited access, a one-way system and a very rough and makeshift ring road to the north of the town.

The harbour

At its southern end the waterfront leads on to the beach of St George's Bay and, to the north, it terminates in the little causeway which unites Palateia island to the mainland. Between lies the broad sweep of a relatively sheltered bay into which project two stone quays. The larger of these accommodates the principal ferries, visiting warships and commercial vessels. There is a bustle of activity when ferries arrive with queues of passengers, vehicles and hotel minibuses. Naxos can even boast a few locals who still meet the boats to call out *domatia* (rooms) to the emerging passengers. With increasing tourism the freelance traveller, seeking rooms on arrival at port, is not now always successful. It is sad that this hardy breed is under threat of extinction. On many islands tour operators have taken up available rooms for the duration of the season. The charm of staying with Greek people in their homes may be a disappearing pleasure.

A small quay adjacent to the larger one is used to tie up those small ferries which are prone to abdicate before the *meltemi*. There is, theoretically, a fast vessel, the *Skopelitis,* which makes a daily journey to Iraklia, Schinoussa, Koufonissia and Amorgos. The weather, however, often intervenes and makes the voyage only marginally more reliable than its predecessor, an ex-Norwegian fiord ship. The attraction of the service is also limited by the knowledge that the return journey cannot be guaranteed any more than the outward run. One beneficial side effect is that this little

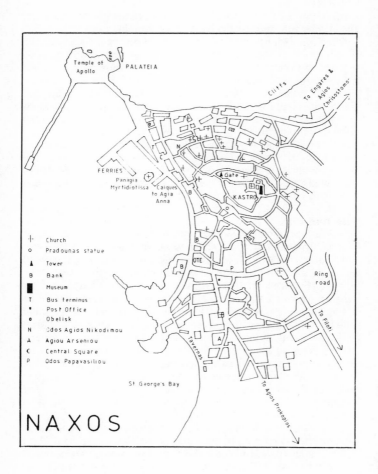

Temple of Apollo

PALATEIA

Cliffs

To Engares & Agios Chrisostomo

FERRIES

Panagia Myrtidiotissa

Caiques to Agia Anna

T

N

Gate

KASTRO

B

B

OTE

P

B

Ring road

To Filoti

A

To Agios Prokopios

St George's Bay

Tavernas

+	Church
o	Pradounas statue
▲	Tower
B	Bank
■	Museum
T	Bus terminus
▪	Post Office
o	Obelisk
N	Odos Agios Nikodimou
A	Agiou Arseniou
C	Central Square
P	Odos Papavasiliou

NAXOS

chain of islands retains its remoteness and genuinely Greek character.

Another small boat, the *Latsos II,* may make the journey on six days of the week to Paroikia and Sifnos. On the other hand it may not. The *Ios* is scheduled to call in en route from Ios to Mykonos but it is packed to capacity when (and if) it arrives.

An excursion ferry, the *Daphne II,* sails on five days of the week to Delos and Mykonos, spending one and a half hours in the former and three hours in the latter. On one day it has been calling first at Piso Livadi in south eastern Paros instead of Delos but journeys such as this are very much dependent on the services required by holiday tour operators.

Caiques leave the jetty at hourly intervals to round the headland of Akrotiri Moungri on the way to Agia Anna, one of the many sandy beaches of western Naxos. This is a most pleasant alternative to the typically packed bus which leaves the nearby waterfront terminus.

The harbour, as in most island ports, is lined with an almost unbroken array of restaurants and cafés with tables both on the pavement and across the road on the harbour side, though the latter may be untenable when the *meltemi* speeds waves against the sea wall. Ferry ticket agencies, a few shops and banks separate the eating places, which are active from early morning to late at night. Certainly Naxos offers a great choice of tavernas to provide variety in eating places if not in the types of meal available.

The waterfront tavernas may not all be among the best on the island but some exude Greekness and nostalgia from every plastic table and chair. The **Kali Kardia** in the centre is simple but typically Greek. A waiter periodically appears to sweep the pavement or a swish of whitewash is spread along the kerb as a precursor to the evening's activity. Nearby, Greeks and tourists savour the aroma of octopus being charcoal grilled in a doorway then taste its dark, diced tentacles washed down with ouzo or retsina.

Above the harbour level some tavernas and cafés enjoy a balcony position, ideally placed to overlook the water and the distant northern shores of Paros. Magnificent sunsets redden the skies behind the hills of Paros as the last rays filter through the swaying silhouettes of the harbour masts. Among these raised restaurants is **Nikos,** probably the best on the island and offering the greatest variety of food. It also spreads from the waterfront balcony through a large and, by island standards, elegant room out on to a broader section of the narrow raised road which parallels the harbour.

Street Arches in Naxos.

The Kastro hill

Naxos, behind the harbour, appears as an intricate maze of tortuous streets, steps and tunnels coating the conical hill of the Kastro. No immediate pattern is evident and this contributes to the element of surprise and the charm of the town. Perhaps it lacks the pristine whiteness and daily coats of paint which adorn the crazed cement patterns and walls of the streets of Mykonos. This is essentially a place where people live and it is still very Greek in atmosphere.

Rooms built over arches and tunnels and decaying wooden doors are a paradise for photographers and painters. White walls trail with bougainvillea and plants everywhere alleviate the white of the buildings. The Greek habit of setting plants in old olive oil cans seems at first glance to indicate a curious lack of artistic sense. However, placed outside the door or on a balcony, window ledge or wall, they mysteriously merge with their surroundings. Only the greenery becomes evident as a foil to the white surrounds. Ubiquitous basil vies with cylindropuntia cactus and the stemmed green rosettes of aeoniums to give pleasure to the eye.

The tramp up to the remains of the Kastro can be undertaken along many different routes. Each is an effort in the heat of the Greek summer but every corner, window and arch repays the effort with visual gems. The dismembered Temple of Apollo has bequeathed marble columns and blocks to a multiplicity of buildings. Gateways especially display an antiquity which is not their own. Eyecatching features are the brass doorknockers fashioned in the form of a hand holding a ball. An example can be seen in the miniature square in front of the Kastro museum on the top of the hill. Although the museum has been closed for many years, it has recently undergone extensive reconstruction and hopefully will be open when you read this book. Its collection includes the Cycladic figurines popularised by a British Museum exhibition as well as Mycenean pottery.

The **Kastro** itself, the walled and fortified heart of Naxos town, was built in the early thirteenth century under the rule of the Venetian, Marco Sanoudo. Materials from earlier structures in the vicinity were used in its construction. However, the ravages of 750 years, including two and a half centuries of Turkish rule, have reduced much of its original massive structure to crumbling foundations. The walls were pierced and gradually replaced by domestic buildings and the tortuous ways which burrow through them. Eventually, the Kastro became virtually indistinguishable from its surroundings.

Today, the Kastro is seen in residual fragments of the walls, gates and towers. The walls, in themselves, are unimpressive but two of the original three gates remain. The site of the south-west gate is on the road just above Pradouna Square. The north-west gate is complete and set in one of the larger sections of the wall. This is striking, with massive stone blocks forming the arch within the grey cleaved slabs of the wall, and it still possesses its enormous old wooden door. It leads through beamed vaults into the Kastro. Alongside the north-west gate is the one surviving cylindrical bastion, the Tower of Glezio. Though not accessible to the public, it is readily visible even from the harbour — a clear reminder of the castle origins of the town.

Thus the pleasures of the ascent are more important than attaining the summit of the Kastro. Although the ascending ways meander without apparent pattern, there are other routes which conform more or less to the contours of the hill. Some are narrow and shady but others broaden out into terraces. One, higher up the hill, accommodates the **Kastro restaurant.** This is not only one of the better eating places but also has a pleasing location with its tables placed around the bust of Christos Pradounas, a local hero of the Macedonian Wars at the turn of the century. The white marble bust is not exceptional but it is mounted on a plinth of rough pieces of emery, mined in the mountains of northern Naxos and almost unique to the island. The same product is set into the base of the small obelisk erected near the northern end of the waterfront to commemorate the dead of the wars of 1912-1922.

Getting the feel of the town

The narrow winding street which follows the lowest level behind the waterfront is a trail of activity. Along its length are many small shops, restaurants, tavernas and bars sheltered from the wind and ideal not only for their food and wine but as places from which to watch the world drift by. The focal point here is the small square between the jetties, shaded by tamarisks and vines and crowded with the tables of a coffee shop and a taverna.

One of the disconcerting features of the bars and cafés used by visitors wishing to practise or improve their Greek language is the inability of the waitress to understand them. The first reaction is to assume that the blank face before them reflects a misplaced stress or eccentricities of the local dialect. The light then dawns that the recipient is more familiar with the dialect of Frankfurt or Paris or Liverpool. Naxos has more than its share of young foreign labour to carry out menial tasks for the summer tourist business. Even before the season begins there is employment in preparing

Naxos: a ball in the hand alongside the museum.

properties for the rush of visitors.

Naxos is beautiful during the baking heat of a summer afternoon when the commercial world closes up and the Greeks retire for the siesta. The bulk of visitors migrate to the beaches and the town is left as a quiet, dappled maze of miniature white canyons for exploration. If the town is at its most alluring at that time, it is most attractive in the evening. At times one suspects that the island has been overtaken by foreigners but the evening reveals the vast influx of mainland Greeks. They parade along the length of the harbour each night through the packed tables of the cafés and restaurants, back and forth, from children in wheelchairs to aged crones and Orthodox priests. The babble of excited conversation at this time in Naxos is usually augmented by the waterfront offices of the Communist Party emitting their nightly programme of propaganda with even greater enthusiasm. Their graffiti of the air seem to fall on deaf Greek ears and deafened north Europeans.

The northern end of town

At the north of the town of Naxos the road to the village of **Engares** emerges and beyond it a rough and little used track to **Apollona**. However, a tramp of little more than a mile along this route from the edge of town leads to the attractive monastic church of **Agios Chrisostomos.** The route affords some impressive views of the storm-swept northwest coast of Naxos. Coarse sandstone and ragged conglomerates of cemented pebbles form a narrow strip bounded by rough cliffs battered and torn by *meltemi* waves. These contrast with the rounded granites and smooth sands of the southwest coast but hardly offer comfortable or safe walking country.

The path to Agios Chrisostomos zig-zags up the hillside and each stop provides a better view back over Naxos town and the straits to Paros. The church is part of an Orthodox nunnery built in the sixteenth century but which has recently undergone extensive repairs. The high white walls resemble the late Venetian castles of the same period and overlook gardens and canes planted below them as an oasis of green amid the dry scrub of the hills.

Around Agios Chrisostomos the granite outcrops as rounded domes, stark and bare, but inviting further investigation. Their gritty surface affords a good foothold and easier climbing than the spiny vegetation of the slopes. Amid these rocks, between the church and the sea, is the chapel of **Agia Irini-Chrissovalandou.** This is a tiny white edifice but looks absolutely marvellous in its steep rocky setting. Grecian chapels are legion. They are constructed with love and a simple artistic flair. Not least of their merits is the choice of location made for them. This is varied and almost inevitably charming, ranging from a bare mountain top site such as Agios Ioannis in the centre of the island to the Naxos harbour islet of Panagia Myrtidiotissa. Agia Irini-Chrissovalandou is not a gem in itself but the small white structure against the granite rock wall and the brilliant blue sky is worth the little effort necessary to reach it.

South of town

The ruggedness of the Naxian landscape immediately to the north of the town is in direct contrast to its southern margin which has smiled on the developer. Its more obvious and immediate assets are gentle slopes, sandy shores and shelter from the blasts of the *meltemi*.

An area of small apartments, rooms and two or three storey hotels has sprung up but has incorporated the Greek ways with plants and the Greek ability to make any site look unfinished no matter how long it has been complete. No Greek town worth its salt lacks a rooftop forest of steel rods projecting from the ferro-concrete structure as a hopeful sign of things to come. Likewise, the road surfaces proffer stone and dust, unfinished concrete or builders' debris in lieu of tarmac. Where these phenomena would be depressing in a wet Salford, they take on a new image in the bright Cycladic light. To the moderate Hellenophile, Greece is not simply a collection of residual Classical antiquities nor is it even a painter's array of white cubic boxes on a yellowed landscape. It combines supreme architectural beauty, attractive decor and ornament with the gaudy and tasteless twentieth-century additions of coloured plastic, glass and concrete.

St George's Bay has long been the popular Greek beach of Naxos but gradually in recent years its indigenous character has been westernised. Tavernas and restaurants have been named and decorated to appeal to northern visitors. Discos augment the traditional Greek amenities and the narrow sandy strand not only forms a playground for Greek families but for European youth. Fortunately the bare breasts of the latter seem to have been taken philosophically by even the older generations of the local people.

The bay is relatively sheltered by the headland of Naxos but there is usually at least enough breeze to make wind surfing a practical proposition. Two schools have boards for hire, the more attractive being the **Flisvos** at the southern limit of the developed beach. This is linked to a taverna and has a windmill style tower on the edge

Naxos: Venetian tower of Glezio.

Destination	Outward	Inward	Fare
Apollona	8.30,10.0,11.0,1.0	6.30,10.30,2.30,5.0,6.0	180
Komiaki	8.30,11.0,1.0	7.0,11.0,3.0,6.30	140
Apiranthos	8.30,11.0,1.0,7.0	7.30,8.45,11.30,3.30,7.0	90
Filoti	8.30,11.0,12.0,1.0	7.0,7.45,9.0,11.45,3.45	65
Chalkio	8.30,11.0,12.0,1.0,7.0	7.05,7.50,9.10,11.50, 3.50,7.20	55
Pirgaki	10.0,11.0,1.0,4.30	10.30,11.30,1.30,5.0	70
Tripodes	10.0,11.0,1.0,4.30	7.30,8.45,10.45,11.45, 1.45, 5.15	35
Melanes	12.0,3.30	7.0,4.0	35
Agia Anna	7.30,9.0,10.0,11.0,12.0 1.0,2.0,3.0,4.0,5.0,6.0, 7.0	8.0,9.30,10.30,11.30, 12.30,1.30,2.30,3.30, 4.30,5.30,6.30,7.30	45
Moutsouna	1.0	6.0	140
Lionas	12.0	6.0	150
Agiasos	12.0	6.0	90
Kinidaros	12.0	7.0	65
Potamia	2.30	7.0	45
Galini	7.30,12.0	8.0,12.30	30
Danakos	12.0	7.0	90
Keramoti	12.0	7.0	115

Table 13   Bus services from Naxos — fares in drachmae

of the sand. Even the turbulent waves of the *meltemi* do not deter the experts here. Their boards are made to leap out of the water spectacularly and at speed on those days when the wind makes the beach untenable for even the most ardent sunbathers.

Beyond the Flisvos taverna urban development gives way to low dunes and quieter shores, the realm of the walkers, the motor cyclists, the jeep and those who do not rate minimal effort and immediate amenities to be of prime significance.

Agios Prokopios and Agia Anna

Those who stay in Naxos may use the beach of St George's Bay but the choice is almost unlimited for the more selective and energetic traveller.

South west of Naxos and St George's Bay projects the pinnacled headland of **Akrotiri Moungri,** rounded by the regular caique service to Agia Anna. The hike to the shore beyond the headland is about 3½ miles (5.6 km). The track follows the beach around the bay initially and, even though the tidal range is only small, it is prone to disappear before the advancing waves. Walkers share this sandy thread with infrequent jeeps and taxis intent on running the gauntlet. Small hired motorbikes similarly generally manage to stay above sand.

The beach track rises on to an embankment carrying the road around the crusty white flats of a saltmarsh behind the bay. Part of this area is now being bulldozed in preparation for a new airport. When this is opened Naxos will inevitably change. The road cuts around the western margins of the flats as a hot and dusty trail. This ascends the gentle incline across the headland in a little valley between low granite ridges. Both of these repay the effort to climb them, not only for the view across the salt flats to Naxos but for the bare granite landscape, peeling and flaking in the blazing daily heat. The ridge on the northern right hand side is surmounted by outcrops deeply and spectacularly pitted by honeycomb weathering.

Curling over the crest of the hill, the dusty trail passes through tiny fields of yellow sheep-grazed stubble to a water hole in the form of a wayside taverna. Like most small and seasonal tavernas, its repertoire is not great and probably half the items listed are off the menu, but the location is right, a halfway house in the heat of the day. Relatively few people raise the energy for the hike and those that do are not only of various nationalities but also of divers character. The Greek proprietors take most things in their stride but have been seen to be openly amused at the sight of youthful Swedes arriving with bare breasts proudly on view while debating whether or not to stop.

The track passes beside a few modern rooms to let and then the way divides, one section carrying on to Agia Anna and the other dropping down to a lagoon sealed off by the beach of Agios Prokopios. The lagoon all but dries up in the summer leaving a fragile saline crust coloured brightly by sundry algae. To most it is a phenomenon for circumnavigating but, in keeping with tourist diversity, an occasional hired Suzuki jeep has been tempted to get across with consequences falling short of the miraculous.

The lagoon sports a tiny taverna on its landward side and others at its northern and southern extremities. Between the lagoon and the sea there are low sand dunes fixed by dispersed tussocks of sunspurge, maritime lilies and carline thistles with scattered junipers. Beyond lies the beach of **Agios Prokopios,** named after the tiny chapel at the head of the lagoon.

The strand is superb. It is made of a quartz grit with particles two to three millimetres across. This is white and clean, comfortable to lie on while not adhering to the skin too readily. As it is made of heavy grains, it resists moving in all but strong winds. It is on the sheltered leeward side of the headland and is a haven during the *meltemi* blasts. Not only is it texturally pleasing but it really is beautiful. It stretches in a gentle arc for two miles from the headland of Akrotiri Prokopios to Agia Anna, plunging fairly rapidly into deep water which appears turquoise over the pale sand. It is never densely crowded even in the height of summer as its population has had to make an effort to get there.

There are, perhaps, an unexpectedly large number of Greeks among the western sun worshippers on this beach and this seems to be indicative of the changing attitude of the Greek population. The concept of a nation closely bound to the Orthodox church, conscious of its ethics and customs and possessing a unique Greekness is gradually being diluted. Greeks, or Athenians in particular, wish to be as sophisticated and progressive as others. Reason rather than accepted tradition is their guide. The merit of living in a sunny climate and sparkling island-studded seas is not lost on them. Black-shrouded women may still accompany the children on to the beaches but it is becoming increasingly the case that younger people will shed their clothes to obtain an unbroken golden hue. Greek tans are beginning to compete with the formidable array of Scandinavian, German, French and British on Aegean shores.

The leeward side of a headland has the merit of providing shelter from the sand blasting. It ensures calm waters in the worst conditions and it also alleviates the problem of jelly fish which the *meltemi* drives onshore from time to time in large quantities in St George's Bay. However, there is one very slight disadvantage here. Offshore winds have the habit of driving the inshore surface water, which has been warmed by contact with the hot sand, out to sea. This is replaced by cooler water welling up from depth. During the windy spells, therefore, the sea appears to be surprisingly cool but it is not unbearable and is a refreshing change from the heat of the beach.

Prokopios beach is not scarred by a multitude of tents nor is it possible for most vehicles to drive along the shores. The only structures are small ephemeral cane wigwams put up for shade by daily visitors or the very few who stay overnight. The canes have been picked from field margins or near the lagoon. They are not unpleasing and change hands or are uprooted and rebuilt by newcomers at regular intervals.

The little chapel of Agios Prokopios is located within a small walled rectangle of enclosed scrub at the foot of the northern headland. It possesses a weatherworn cane awning but architecturally is not exceptional. However, it is crowned by a small belfry arch, inside which is suspended a brass bell coated with a green patina. Inscribed on the bell quite clearly is RHYL 1940; presumably it was recovered from a British ship of that name sunk locally during the Second World War.

Granite projects as a low sharp headland to the west of the chapel and behind it rises a conical hill covered with thorny pads and thickets and crowned by steeper rocky outcrops. Its windswept summit affords views for miles around and its crags and cliffs are strikingly different from the granites below. Instead of the latter's typically rough and gritty surface, these rocks are smooth, in places almost glassy. They are pale, even white in places, with banding picked out in ochre and red colours. This is a lava flow of rhyolite matching almost precisely similar conical hills in eastern Paros.

The slopes of the hill sweep down on the northern side to the multiple points of Akrotiri Moungri. Unlike the granite areas, the cliffs are steep and the rocks are a rambling mass of sandstones and pebbly conglomerates. The coast is quiet and ruggedly attractive but the cliff tops are dangerous and the few beaches stony and wave-lashed.

Agia Anna itself lies at the southern end of the Prokopios beach where a smaller granite headland projects into the Naxos channel.

Like so many prominent relief features, it is capped by a tiny chapel. The hamlet itself is not attractive. It possesses a taverna on either side of the dirt track which serves the jetty. The facilities and the staff are overworked by the summer crowds so that it lacks the natural charm of both Greek people and places.

The cause of Agia Anna is not helped by its dual role of tourist centre and commercial port. The regular flow of tourist traffic by caique and bus from Naxos, each offering an hourly service during summer days, is mildly in conflict with the smaller inter-island ships and the tractor-drawn wagons which link up with them. Bricks, cement and other building materials are inward bound for the gradual development of apartments and rooms, but more significant is the outward-bound traffic in agricultural produce, notably potatoes. Agia Anna is backed by the plain of Livadi, one of the most extensive areas of flat cultivated land on the island.

The main problem of Agia Anna is the attraction of the sandy beach which arcs southward from the chapel point. This is a three-mile stretch approached either by the road to Agia Anna or by another track in a midway position at Plaka. The sand has a finer texture than Prokopios and is a facade to a fairly extensive area of low dunes.

The focus of attention is the camp site located nearly a mile away from the jetty in the midst of the sandy wastes. The vastness of the area and its relative remoteness as well as its sheltered attractive sands have made it a mecca for many more than the official campers. Young people see it as a beautiful and wild area in which they can lead a beautiful and 'natural' life. Cane shelters have sprung up everywhere to accommodate the beadmakers, guitar players, surfers and the many who unselfconsciously while away their hours naked in the sun.

The ideal is fine but unfortunately the beautiful people and the idyllic life in the sun are not matched by cooking and washing facilities, by sanitation and waste disposal. Perhaps the majority are conscious of its limitations and manage to keep their piece of heaven unsullied but, inevitably, the place in the sun turns into a place in the slum under a welter of coke cans, plastic bags, bottles, paper and cigarette ends. However, the extent of the Agia Anna sands does mean that it is possible to outdistance the crowds and to appreciate both the setting and the sun.

The attitude of the Greek population is remarkably tolerant. A notice at the harbour of Agia Anna proclaims 'No nudism' and this is true in the immediate environs of the sign but carries no weight little more than a hundred metres away. More remarkable and amusing are the little old men on donkey back with panniers bulging under the weight of local pears, grapes and water melons. They drift among the sunbathers on the beach calling out *'Stafelia! Karpouzi!'* Their approach to customers is cheerful and pleasant and their sales technique would fit equally well in a little local shop. It is as though cutting slices of water melon and handing them to beautiful bare-breasted or totally naked girls and boys had been their experience from birth. They are seemingly oblivious to the attributes of youth and always charming.

Heading south: Naxos to Pyrgaki

A bus service runs south from Naxos to Pyrgaki on the southwest corner of the island but it is infrequent and restricting as a means of exploring. At a cost of about £5 per day it is possible to hire an automatic small motor bike without need of licence or hard hat. (Costs are greater but regulations equally lax on more powerful machines.) This gives access to the nooks and crannies of the coast or leads to places where the feet must take over.

The route crosses the green plain of Livadi, running through high walls of cane. A band of low hills separates Livadi from the southwestern lowlands and the road climbs over them linking a chain of villages on the way. **Glinado** and **Agios Arsenios** are quiet agricultural communities which alter little with time. The third village, **Tripodes,** is more attractive to the eye.

Names can be confusing. At the roadside a sign clearly indicates the village to be Vivlos though local maps beg to differ. Vivlos is the name given to the former municipality of which Tripodes was the main village. At one time the area was noted for its wine production though this is no longer of great significance. Today, the current name is self-explanatory when the village is visited. The site is an attractive and green hillslope on which the white cubic houses leave streets with marble flags in cool shade. Above the village and emphasised by a steep-sided little valley cut into one flank, is a rocky ridge surmounted by three 'pods' in the form of three windmills. These are incomplete but, set against the rocks, oleander bushes and the valley cultivated for tomatoes and melons, it is a picture.

Out of Tripodes, the road passes over fairly open moorland on rounded hills with dry stone walls delineating the fields. Here and there white outcrops of rock peep through the stony brown earth to reveal marble, a surprising rarity in the geology of Britain but quite commonplace in some of the islands of the Cyclades.

The road, having surmounted the hill crest, straightens out and makes a graded descent over about three miles back to sea level. It gradually converges upon the coast of **Alyko** though there are dirt roads leading to the shore before that, notably at **Kastraki.** Some visitors could consider leaving the bus at Kastraki and walking the half mile to the quite magnificent and near deserted shore.

The Kastraki beach forms one long, low sandy sweep from the granite promontory of **Mikri Vigla** in the north to the low flat headlands of **Anagli** and **Kouroupias** in the south. It is on to this southern headland that a spur road leads to the imaginary resort of Alyko. It terminates in the extensive and ghostly concrete shell of a tourist development that has never come to fruition. The dark hollow chambers rest in the midst of a scrub land of junipers and low pines, remote and unserviced. It even lacks the twentieth century vandals to turn it into a crumbling ruin like so many unoccupied buildings. This is a modern folly and a monument to the slow pace of change in less accessible Greek islands.

Perhaps one reason for its demise is the land on which it stands. The headland has a margin of low cliffs and rocky slopes, about three to four metres high. Though these are of granite, they have been subjected here to processes of geological decay and are crumbling and gritty. They are not comfortable to sit or to climb on and lack both magnificence and beauty. Like granites everywhere, however, when they decay, quartz crystals are liberated from the matrix of pale clay minerals to form white sand. Although only postage stamp coves of sand separate the grey granite buttresses around the Alyko promontory, these granites have contributed to the vast stretches of sand at Kastraki to the north and Pyrgaki to the south.

The road beyond Alyko crosses the arid flats of **Potamides** and the beautiful wide sandy beaches which lie adjacent to them. A solitary small taverna stands in the shade of the olives at the roadside, a watering hole in a provisionless land. The open sands have been swept by winds up the slopes on the southeast side of the bay and fingers of white push into the shade of twisted junipers which cling to the hillside. Small rounded rocks are exposed as the sand moves on. This also is a grey and white banded marble, baked and crystallised by the nearby granite.

The southern road, having been frayed and stony in patches for a number of miles, deteriorates on reaching **Pyrgaki.** Here, the same developers as at Alyko have attempted to launch a complex

Headland of Mikri Vigla.

of rooms and apartments around a central facility. At its inception a number of years ago, this looked as though it would be successful but time has seen it slowly decay as its potential has not been realised. Even the beach attracts relatively few, not because of its own failings but due to the lack of amenities around.

Mikri Vigla
The terminus of the road may be something of a non-event but the journey south need not be cast entirely in the same mould. Three and a half miles north of Pyrgaki on the road back to Naxos is a turnoff which leads to **Mikri Vigla** (Cape Little Lookout), one of the most pleasing parts of the Naxian landscape and well worth any trouble entailed in attempting to reach it.

The dirt track pitches off at a steep angle, rutted by vehicles and furrowed by the rains of winter. It is also hot and dusty in summer. Beside the road is the little chapel of Agia Paraskevi and beyond it, set back from both the headland and the shore, is the handful of houses and apartments of the hamlet of Mikri Vigla.

The track crosses a similar one at a soft and sandy place. This crossroads offers access to the south side of the headland to the left and the north side to the right. Straight ahead the route gradually peters out but rises on to the flanks of the point.

If the southern route is followed, then at a very short distance the track opens out on to hard salt flats which can be used for parking. A few yards of low sand hills separate the flats from the northern end of Kastraki Bay. The sandy beach is immense and virtually empty. A taverna stands at this point and, within two hundred metres, all of the beach population. The conical peak of the cape of Mikri Vigla shelters the beach and protects the few wind surfers from the ravages of the *meltemi*.

The gritty track to the right leads northward parallel to the coast. The path looks down through dark junipers on to a beach of glowing, coarse sand. It pitches steeply into the water in contrast to the gently shelving strand at Kastraki. The warm gold colour shimmers through the transparent sea as a brilliant and enticing turquoise, darkening with depth into navy blue.

A handful of people rest under the shade of the junipers and periodically plunge into the sea. As at Prokopios, the water and the beach are perpetually alluring and ablaze with colour, a considerable contrast with the sometimes grey outlook of the less clean and overpopulated sands of Agia Anna a couple of miles to the north.

The road is suitable for vehicles for only a short distance before

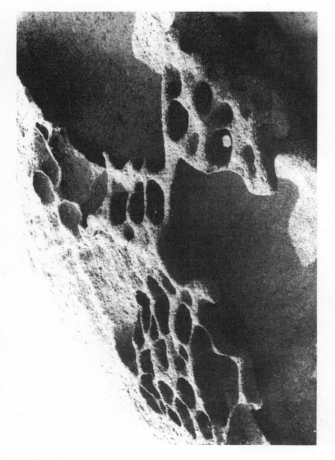

Honeycomb tracery in Mikri Vigla's granite.

it comes to an abrupt end. Thereafter even a footpath becomes difficult to discern across the gently sloping scrubland between the foot of the hills and the low cliffed coast. Its quietness and emptiness in itself is pleasing, especially where the slopes have been furrowed deeply by a winter stream. This opens out into a tiny sand embayment overlooked by junipers and agaves and wedged between grey cliffs, a haven in this miniature wilderness. A little way past this point, the hills recede from the coast and a small taverna marks the southern limits of **Plaka** beach.

Pleasant though this tract of coast is, the real magnet of this area is to be found by following the track ahead to Mikri Vigla, a wide cone of rock projecting above a ten-metre platform.

The isthmus of the headland has had sand drifted across it from Kastraki to the south and from the Bay of Kyrades to the north. The track is soft and sandy at this point and is surrounded by taller shady junipers with gnarled trunks. The vegetation here is sparse not only because of the blowing sand but because of a herd of goats which jingles across its wastes. Its brown and fawn members eat their way through everything and scatter when approached to pose impressively on the summits of rocky crags.

Even in the height of summer this area is not crowded, partly because of its difficulty of access and also because of the total lack of developed amenities. It appeals to those who do not mind making the effort to attain solitude or a wilder landscape. There are those who trek on foot, a few that come on motor cycles and others armed with more rugged vehicles such as VW vans and Japanese jeeps. These provide havens for the few who stay to enjoy this marvellous setting. Hopefully, the slow progress of tourism in other parts of Naxos and the salutary failure of the Alyko enterprise may deter the developer from making inroads into Mikri Vigla.

The headland is made up of a hill of almost bare rock with a low plateau circling it on three sides. A few thistles, sparse grasses and junipers cover the surface of the lower land but there is a remarkable exposure of unvegetated rock in the low cliffs and slopes leading down into the sea.

Granite is a curiously variable rock. In some cases it appears tough and resistant, enduring unchanged for an eternity. In others, some of its mineral components undergo a chemical alteration induced either by internal reactions or by surface weathering processes. This results in decay and breakdown so that the rock whitens as kaolin develops. The shaping of its landscape is also controlled by the patter of its rectilinear jointing. These weaknesses provide the access for weathering agents to attack the mass and

Mikri Vigla: spherical granite cores

Kolymbithres: weathered granite mushroom.

it is their distribution, therefore, which determines the curious forms which are left. In some places the joints are close packed but in others their absence leaves massive faces of unbroken rock. In either case at Mikri Vigla, weathering creates a variety of fascinating forms.

The tors of Dartmoor owe their origin to the same characteristics but on Naxos the processes are both more visible and more advanced. The rectangular blocks are stacked at the northwest corner of the headland like massive masonry but, here and there, they have been reduced to rounded cores and even to residual spheres like gigantic cannon balls.

On the south-facing slopes, even where the jointing is not strikingly in evidence, the bare golden rock has started to weather into domes and ellipses. The daily roasting by the Aegean sun expands the surface and helps to peel off another flake from the cooler core, Salt spray, too, makes its contribution to the breakdown and causes the delicate fretwork effect of honeycomb weathering.

To appear in print or on film may spell the end for any paradise. Certainly it cannot remain unchanged if publicity attracts attention and lots more visitors. These, in turn, promote improved access and transport. As yet, it is possible for a solitary camper to set up a tiny tent on the edge of the boulder-strewn cone of Mikri Vigla. It is a different world. It could be an African *inselberg,* an island of rocks projecting from the veld.

If the serried ranks of north Europeans have not yet discovered every gem in the Greek landscape, sheep and goats almost certainly have. A flock of sheep shuffle in the shadows of the steeper rocks, a pool of darkness in the glowing granite. They wallow in the cool shade, temporarily oblivious to the singular lack of edible plants. They have not encountered harrassment from humans and appreciate Mikri Vigla's solitude like the discerning traveller.

Apollona via Chalkio, Filoti and Apiranthos

The longest route emerging from Naxos town is that to the northernmost corner of the island and to the little harbour of Apollona. The total distance amounts to 31 miles (50 km) but, as the road crosses the central mountain system, it pursues a meandering course over the ridges and down the valleys. The quality of the highway is, to put it kindly, rather variable and what to the inexperienced appears to be a short trip proves to be a major event.

Japanese jeeps, motor cycles and automatic 50cc bikes can be hired for travel, though the latter would prove inadequate over the gradients and distance. Filling stations are thin on the ground. In fact, apart from those in Naxos town, there is only one other at the central village of Filoti.

Alternatively there are two possible bus services. One is the regular bus which leaves the Naxos harbour terminal three times a day for Apollona. Like all Greek island services this is almost inevitably crowded. At some times the packing of passengers is unbelievable and yet the conductor's task of collecting fares is carried out where any movement seems impossible. Retrieving dropped coins may pose problems that are less easily overcome. This route connects the string of villages across the centre of the island to the town of Naxos. It is the lifeline of the island.

The alternative is a tour bus which departs from the southern end of the waterfront each morning at 9.30 am. This coach is fairly spacious and pleasant and makes stops at Chalkio and Apiranthos on the outward journey and at Filoti on the return. It is not a lot more expensive than the regular service and is worth using for the breathing space on board that it provides. There is a courier who gives a commentary in Greek and English on the passing scene. It is clear and understandable and a must for those who like to be in touch with the location of the technological high school, the number of chapels, and the total population of each village.

The disadvantage of the tour bus lies in the limitation that it makes on the time to be spent at any location. However, the normal bus service is so infrequent that it, too, is very restricting. Perhaps the tour bus can give this overall picture and the regular service be selected for closer examination of features that appeal to individuals.

The Potamias

The route followed crosses the plain of Livadi then separates from the southern highway as the climb into the hills begins through the little village of **Galanado.** The landscape here is relatively green and the massive granite rocks of the coast change to more sparse tabular slabs poking through the grazing.

As the road ascends so the relative relief and beauty of the Naxian hills springs into evidence. North of the road the headwaters of the Peritsis river have carved a deep and green valley into the rocky uplands. Its flanks are terraced like a Javanese hillside and the floor has olive and almond trees amid the vineyards. The three little

115

hamlets of **Kato, Mesi** and **Ano Potamia** (Lower, Middle and Upper Potamia) line its flanks in what may well be the prettiest rural location on the island.

Should you want to take a closer look at the valley the only way is to hire a motor cycle, jeep or buggy — although there is a solitary bus leaving Naxos at 2.30 pm and returning at 7 pm. The dirt road slides down towards the valley floor after branching off the route to Melanes. The yellowed grasses and barren terraces of the steep slopes contrast with the green world of swaying canes, twisted olives and pillar cypress below them.

Even in the parched height of summer water trickles in the brook which links the Potamias. Each village is an oasis of peace. The road follows the valley side above them and the only noises are the clatter of donkeys' hooves and the voices of playing children. There are no amenities for foreigners such as shops, garages or cafés but there is a little idyllic piece of unaltered rural Greece. Each little path between the white buildings is a trench of cool shade with pools of sunlight illuminating trailing vines and walls of draped mesembryanthemums.

Mesi Potamia possesses a prominent church just a little way off the road. It has a small but attractive walled courtyard and a eucalyptus to bathe it in dappled shadows. Ano Potamia lies on the opposite side of the valley, a smaller cluster of houses but penetrated by the road and having a central open space beside a restaurant. This can provide a cool drink at the end of the Potamia trail in a garden of convolvulus, oranges and aloes. By way of a change from its normal blissful peace, Saturday night sees this setting enlivened by flowing wines and strident bouzoukis catering for Naxian visitors.

The pull out of the Potamias emphasises its uniqueness. Once away from the range of life giving water the cypresses and fruit trees are replaced by a boulder strewn wilderness. Great slabs of gneiss decorate the harsh upland surface as the equally rocky road threads its way to Chalkio.

An alternative route

An alternative and parallel route to the valley of the Potamias lies to the north on another dirt road. This branch first connects with the tiny steep hamlet of **Agios Thaleleos** and then with **Kourounochori.** Here there is the well preserved and beautifully located Venetian tower of Pyrgos Mavrogeni looking across the vale to Agios Apostoli. The tapering square bastion is typical of others on the island but unfortunately its preservation has been accompanied by incongruous modern window frames and a television aerial on the roof.

From Kourounochori the rough path leads down to the site of one of the island's three *kouroi* (statues) on the valley floor amid the clustered canes, cypress, pines and oleander. In the midst of the greenery there is a large walled garden enclosing neatly tilled tan earth and a prolific growth of dahlias, maize, melons, lemons, oranges, peaches, apples and pears. In the centre, a walled goldfish tank is supplied with water via an original ladder bucket system from the irrigation well. The same dark watery depths refrigerate the drinks supply of this Garden of Eden.

The *kouros* was being excavated from the marble walls of the valley close by when its leg was broken and the project was abandoned at an advanced stage of development. The grey figure lies forlornly in its little stone walled enclosure but it is probably a greater attraction now in this lovely setting than it would have been had the task been completed.

The way from the *kouros* emerges from the plumose cypress and green bushy heads of stone pines. It reaches a similar wilderness to that above Ano Potamia and then continues through the village of **Kinidaros** whose population is dependent upon the vast white-walled marble quarries on its southern side. This road reaches the Apollona highway between Apiranthos and Koronos thus missing out the three large villages of Chalkio, Filoti and Apiranthos.

Chalkio and Filoti

Returning to the main road to Apollona, it swings south away from the Potamia valley to approach the hamlet of **Sangri.** Nearby, on one of the windswept summits to the north stands **Pano Kastro,** the High Castle. This is a hillfort occupied from Hellenistic times through the Venetian period of the early Middle Ages rather like Old Sarum at Salisbury.

The village of **Chalkio** lies astride and constricts the highway, inviting further investigation. It is set on the floor of the Tragea valley in the middle of a mass of olive trees, but the richness of its setting is not reflected in evident prosperity in the village, which sems to display a reluctance to be involved in a modern highway and its uninvited traffic. Its population are not, like many Greeks, outgoing and interested, its side roads are quiet, and its Venetian castle continues its prolonged process of slow decay, seldom disturbed even by the shutter of a visitor's camera. The central church defies the artistic spirit of a photographer in its welter of poles and wires. Only a telephoto from the steps of the castle can penetrate the net! Opposite the church, the sidestreet leads to the quiet little square of the village. A huge and solitary tree covers it almost from wall to wall and shades the tables of Chalkio's restaurant. An adjacent building displays a corner of ornately carved projecting corbels, beautiful in themselves but now no longer supporting a superstructure for which they were designed.

Less than two miles from Chalkio stands **Filoti,** the largest of the island's villages, still within the green sward of the Tragea valley. The road climbs past still active marble quarries towards Filoti. The same rocks dominate the mountains to the north, their bare courses prominent on the valley sides like ribs curving from the craggy backbone of the mountain ridge. Even within the town, building operations reveal the same beautiful material, here banded in shades of dove grey.

By contrast, Filoti is a bustling place; it never seems still. In keeping with its filling station, vehicles appear out of nowhere. By the plane trees in the centre there are bars and restaurants and people waiting endlessly for the arrival of the bus. The aged sages while away the hours clicking their *komboloi* (worry beads), clacking their backgammon boards and watching the world go by.

Filoti is on a mountainside with the high road passing through it straight and gradually ascending to escape the confines of the valley. The small roads of the village rise steeply on one side of the main road and fall away on the other. This type of site produces a multitude of quaint stairways, gateways and arches, though not on the scale of Naxos itself.

A central feature on the hillside is the silver-domed church of the Assumption, the focus of the festival on 15 August. Religious festivals throughout the world attract many faithful and hordes of onlookers. In some cases it is a moving experience for all concerned, as on St Spyridon's Day in Corfu. There the mummified remains of the saint are carried in a vertical casket over the prostrate forms in the streets of those seeking a miracle cure. The result is a desperate scrummage not only in the streets but, later, in the church where the multitude fight to kiss the blackened foot of the saint. The struggle, the anger, the devotion and the forlorn hopes of the afflicted cannot fail to stir the onlooker.

Filoti's festival is not quite like that. At night it comes to life. The population descends on the village from the hills around and even streams out of Naxos itself. The village is impassable to traffic. The approaches are lined with parked vehicles and the road is packed solid with people. The scene is certainly not one of religious fervour but of people bent on having a good time. The restaurants are working flat out as the charcoal grills turn out the lamb cutlets to match the production line flow of chips. A seat is at a premium and so, too, is service. A few words of Greek and a little confidence are essential to securing a supply of retsina and solid sustenance. There is not really room for the more exotic and allegedly typical features of Greek revelry. Glasses and plates are not dashed to the ground and spontaneous dancing is not a free for all. A family group pays for its bouzouki accompaniment and dances fairly sedately in circles, clad in best suits but with evident enjoyment and lack of self consciousness. With the right company the visitors can enjoy the experience. Most who venture into such situations are confirmed Hellenophiles anyway and the Greekness of the evening is sufficient.

Progressing beyond Filoti, there is a bare rock ridge with steep marble walls on the right of the road. Its crest, unbelievably, is crowned with the little white chapel of Agios Ioannis. There seems no limit to the dedication of the Greeks to their Orthodox church.

Two or three hairpin bends farther on at about two kilometres from Filoti, a small green gully crosses the road at the nearest point to the island's highest mountain, **Mt Zas** (1004 metres). It provides a challenge to some though hardly involving a feat of Alpine daring.

Climbing Mt Zas

The gully is followed upwards by a rough track which gives hope of an ordered ascent through the notoriously spiny vegetation which covers most Mediterranean mountains. The hope is short lived as the track leads into walled and terraced orchards of vines, figs and olives. Every aperture is sealed off by walls, wires and ubiquitous thorn stacks. It is not the sole aim of local farmers to obstruct would-be climbers though they certainly lack enthusiasm for intruders. The barricades are anti-goat defences and are evidently much needed.

The solution is to turn left off the track at less than a hundred metres from the road into a derelict olive orchard with oak trees bearing enormous dark galls. The former terraces have been devastated by the hooves and appetites of the goats. Terrace walls are broken down and the dusty earth exposed. The only greenery to survive is that of sprays of poisonous sapped stem euphorbias and the bright berry heads of cuckoo pints.

Climbing through the degraded terraces leads to a spur on the western side of the gully. Here, rock outcrops reduce the possibility of the land being taken up for agriculture. The next section is a trying one. Climbing is not a struggle against steep slopes, rock walls or excessive heat but the tortured effort of avoiding the scratching thorns which abound everywhere. Shorts and trainers are ideal in most respects for climbing here but they are not thorn proof. The easier routes follow outcropping slabs of sparkling mica schist between the furry pads of tall growing verbascum.

As the skyline ridge is reached the vegetation thins and the slope levels out. Dry stone walled enclosures are crowded with goats, brown and buff, black and grey, horned and hornless with bells jangling to announce their presence. Beside their dusty paddocks are cleared areas with a thin yellow stubble of grain.

A view across a shallow gully, laced by goat trails through its spiny pads, presents the main ridge of Zas. A stone wall with wire mesh on top follows the base of the ridge and can be crossed where there is a kink in the line of the wall. Over this there is a bouldery scree slope of water fluted limestones which gives access to the bare rock surfaces of the Zas escarpment.

A little platform overlooks the massive rocky western face of Zas and the fretwork of toothed limestone crags which fringe the summit above the startling drop to the west. As is usually the case, the effort seems worth while once on the top. The sky is blue and the sun is shining but it is remarkably cool even in the heat of the day. The views are stunning. The mountain is seen as a great white wall of limestone facing west and rising out of inclines of pale barren scree. Small dark trees pockmark the white in seemingly impossible growth conditions. Closer inspection shows these to be small leathery-leaved maples complete with winged seeds *(Acer monspessulanum)*.

Chalkio, Filoti and Apiranthos are spread below in their more verdant cloak and the scars of marble quarrying are evident below Filoti and at Kinidaros. The background shows Paros in the Cycladean haze. To the north east the mountain's dip slope falls away more gradually but the bay of Moutsouna can be distinguished and, to the south, the twisting dusty trail to Chimarrou across the mountains in front of the dark backdrop of Amorgos.

The climb, the view and the solitude all add to the elation of the ascent of Zas but it is not for everyone and the mountain can be viewed in comfort from the road to Apollona above Filoti.

Apiranthos

Having escaped from the Tragea valley, the road remains at a high level in a green land and is lined with white marble outcrops stained red by the terra rossa soils. In a short distance it climbs a little more to reach the village of **Apiranthos,** one of the most pleasant on the island.

Apiranthos is not really geared to catering for tourists. Its amenities are minimal but its charm is considerable. The bus stops where the road flattens out and widens beside the parish church of the Assumption. Here, there is a view over the hillside olive groves on one side and, on the other, the narrow stone paved road which forms the high street of the village. A tiny store and snack bar lie adjacent to the church and spell out the facilities for visitors. Broad steps climb up from the paved road and a glimpse of baggy pantaloons on an aged inhabitant give an indication of the quiet backwater that Apiranthos has remained even to the present day. Similarly a walk through the village will reveal women weaving on a loom by an open door or window. The inhabitants have not become weary of curious visitors nor are they intent upon relieving them of their money. They are happy and friendly and typically Greek. The passer-by is still likely to be invited to watch the loom at work or to be asked where they come from — *Apo pou iste?* — in friendly curiosity.

The island of Naxos is hardly a mecca for those in pursuit of serious archaeology. Much that has been discovered on the islands in general has been whisked away to the National Museum in Athens or to collections abroad. Only Iraklion can boast a major collection outside the capital. Nevertheless, there are small museums elsewhere. One is in Naxos town at the summit of the Kastro. Another is housed in a little terraced property with its door on the main street of Apiranthos. It is evident from the relatively slender number of artifacts available that Naxian culture extends back to and is contemporary with Minoan civilisation in Crete as early as 4000 BC. The remains are in the form of megaliths, some inscribed, a considerable amount of pottery, painted or marked with coil patterns, and the curious figurines or idols. The whole is represented in Apiranthos and is a part of the Cycladic culture which has been exhibited at the British Museum.

A tiny shady square is located on the main street of Apiranthos and in it a few benches, chairs and tables invite travellers to pause for a drink from the café, to exchange words with the locals or to investigate and photograph the adjacent archways. The town is clean and attractive encouraging side tracks to picture a doorway, a plant or painted spiral steps. It is then that its superficial simplicity is lost in a maze of byways and arches and it is easy to get lost without really trying.

The kouros at Apollona, large, rough hewn and unfinished.

On to Apollona

The route followed from Apiranthos to Apollona is long and tortuous and close to the watershed between the western and eastern slopes of the island. It is a high, green land of steep-sided valleys shrouded on evergreen oaks and olives with patches of cultivation. The villages of **Koronos, Skado** and **Koronida** cling to the steep mountain sides and are commonly gloomier than other parts of the island. This is due to the cap of cloud which clings to the summits fed by the moisture whipped up by the *meltemi.* They are also shrouded in the economic gloom of unemployment because mining and quarrying have gradually been eliminated as sources of revenue.

From Koronida there is a sinuous descent to Apollona. The road utilises a fairly straight valley with a small rocky gorge at its base. Apollona is visible as a white patch in the distance, wedged between the northern headlands. It is little over 30 miles (50 km) from Naxos but slow progress enforced by gradients, curves and a locally grim road surface make it seem further.

Just above the village, a red dirt track leads off to the west and is signposted to the **Kouros,** a phenomenon almost unique to Naxos. The road climbs between small outcrops of white marble and affords a good view over Apollona. Steps lead up the slope on the left and emerge on a small paved platform beside the *kouros.* This is a statue 10.5 metres long, inclined from the strata of marble from which it was being carved at an angle of about 30°.

The statue is believed to date from the Classical Period of Greek civilisation in the sixth century BC. It may be of Apollo or Dionyssos. Certainly it lacks detail for precise identification as does the similar, but smaller, *kouros* located in Flerio, north of the Potamia valley.

The principle of its creation seems to be similar to the multitude of obelisks carved from granite in Egypt but, unlike those, its excavation and extraction from the solid rock posed unforeseen problems. A view of the marble outcropping around the *kouros* shows that it is closely jointed and weathers into a pseudo-karstic scenery like Pennine limestones. Such joints cut across the massive recrystallised marble beds and must have posed a persistent problem to the classical masons. Favouring them was the relative softness of the marble in comparison to granites. Chiselled furrows rib the trench cut around the statue as a memorial to the stamina and skill of the early Naxiot workers.

The *kouros* is imposing even in its unfinished state, The great grey giant, felled and petrified, reclines with an arm raised, a perpetual and ominous figure from the past waiting for the future.

It is possible to trek down into **Apollona** from the *kouros* through the fields and past the tethered goats. At the same time the little track opens out on to the cliffs on the windswept north side of the village and looks down on the surf pounding up the stony beach. The base of the cliffs is lashed by foam and below lies a glimpse of turquoise in the water to attract not only the visitor but also the local rod and line fishermen.

The path enters the village close beside its central feature, the church. This is large and relatively modern but it is visible from quite a distance away, not least because of the bright blue dome crowning its white walls. Unlike many of the beautiful churches and chapels, this is bright inside and worth a diversion to look at its shining gilded icons.

Apart from its historical associations, Apollona has started to grow as a resort because it is quiet in comparison to Naxos. It also attracts because of the sandy beach on its sheltered southeastern side. This pitches more steeply into the sea than the Agios Georgios beach of Naxos and is scenically more imposing because of the high steep headlands which enclose it. Its distant and relatively inaccessible location may attract some but will almost certainly deter others, especially as there is no regular link by sea. Although property has developed a little back from the beach up the lowland flats of the valley, it may well have reached the limits of its commercial possibilities. The small waterfront development is not typical of Greek harbours. The wooden awnings and frames could be in any western resort but, between these and the church, a little restaurant raised above the waterfront can provide retsina and fish to make Apollona seem a pot of gold at the end of a rainbow.

Sidetracks to Moutsouna and Lionas

Apiranthos is at an altitude of over 500 metres and from it an allegedly paved road descends from the Naxos to Apollona route to reach the east coast at Moutsouna.

Local maps indicate this to be a journey of a little over four miles each way along a fairly straight route. This provides a lesson for travellers intent upon exercising their map-reading skills on the fairly attractive tourist maps available in Naxos (or indeed in other parts of Greece). The relatively straight-looking route along the Ellas valley actually covers about seven miles and becomes tortuous with hairpin sections. Incidentally, Greek maps also pose problems when ways branch or intersect, especially on unsurfaced roads. Signposts are a rarity. Branches that one anticipates from the map appear not to exist but others appear where none are expected.

Much, of course, depends upon the means of transport available for the journey. Regular, or irregular, bus services are present along few routes and it would not do to rely on taxis. One might foresee a taxi being available at Apiranthos and one would be wrong. Motor cycles are almost universally available and neither the lack of a driving licence nor a helmet need prove a deterrent. However, the state of the roads may overcome even the audacious, especially over long distances.

The energetic can set out for destinations such as Moutsouna on foot. Hitch-hiking will only be possible with exceptional luck as cars are few and far between and those that exist are commonly packed with people bound for the coast. In the case of Moutsouna, the hiker must remember that the outward journey from Apiranthos is a gradual descent and that the seven miles back entail a continuous, wearying climb.

The road initially is encouraging tarmac shaded by evergreen oaks. These sport acorns encased in long fibred cups, each looking like a large egg in a bird's nest. Drought-resisting euphorbias sprout at the roadside and dark red earth mantles the silvery lustrous surfaces of schist exposed by engineering works. By Cycladic standards this is a green and pleasant land.

A little way down the road, the tarmac terminates for a short distance and, although it reappears, it is interrupted by stony or rutted and furrowed sections.

The schist layers alternate with marble, most white but some with grey banding. In places at the roadside it has been quarried for roadworks and building. The quarry faces reveal that rainwater has trickled down the joints in the marble, gradually dissolving it away to form iron stained cavities. The same lime-charged water has precipitated its burden on other faces in the form of fluted sheets and ribs. This stalactite bas-relief is stained rust red by the downwash from the overlying soil and then cast into three dimensions by the brilliant light and shade.

Where the road switches back and forth to descend steeper slopes, one is tempted to shortcut across the bends, scrambling over the loose and rocking marble debris, and picking a way between the yellowed carline thistles and uninviting spiny shrubs. One of the more surprising characteristics of the Greek wildernesses is the lack of visible wild life. Birds are few and far between and so are mammals, rodents and snakes. Even the lizards seem sparse in number and variety on Naxos.

The paucity of visible organisms is not limited to land locations such as this. The same is true of the shallow coastal waters. Whereas the shores of cooler north European seas are rich in a fauna of shellfish, the Cycladic Aegean appears almost devoid of them. Beachcombing is not for shells here. This surprising situation may possibly result from the activities of volcanoes such as Milos and Santorini. The vast outfall of ash and its enormous spread may well have buried such creatures beyond their ability to burrow out and thus annihilated large populations. Migration and colonisation from other areas can be a slow process.

Moutsouna

At rather over half way to Moutsouna the road is joined by a brand new tarmac way which emerges from a dry and rocky valley to the north. There is no traffic and no wear on the road and the reason for its existence is not immediately obvious. It is the result of an unfortunate misinterpretation of the economic situation.

The hill region north of this location, and especially towards Koronos and Skado, is rich in the mineral emery. This is an uncommon material, a mixture of oxides of aluminium and iron, closely related to corundum. It has been worked extensively only at Kayabachi in Turkey and here in Naxos and is associated with the metamorphism of shales and limestones by the great, formerly molten, granites. It occurs as lenses and aggregates in the schists and marbles and has not only been mined actively but has been picked out by farmers and landowners in many parts of the island. In fact, a fairly common feature are the little piles of black stones built up at road and field side by local workers. These are mounds of emery, collected with a view to future sale.

The main producing centres for emery were connected across the mountains to the port facilities at Moutsouna by an aerial ropeway but eventually the road was built to connect workings on this slope to the coast. The aerial ropeway is still in position and, a little farther down the hill, it comes into view with its rusting and laden cradles swinging in the wind but otherwise immobile.

The reason for working emery was its property of hardness; it is one of the hardest minerals available for industry as an abrasive. This is tougher than the quartz commonly used on glass papers but less hard than industrial diamonds. However, the difficulties of mining and transportation as well as the world limitations on its availability have resulted in industry looking elsewhere for materials, notably in man-made compositions such as tungsten

Emery train at Moutsouna, fully loaded but going nowhere.

carbide. The consequence has been the collapse of emery mining.

The last few yards of descent into **Moutsouna** show its newer face as a small collection of holiday homes for Athenians and others able to afford and reach this location. A couple of rather inactive cafés look out to sea across these slopes and almost one hundred per cent of the people here are Greek. North Europeans have not been inclined or encouraged to investigate its possibilities. In any case its industrial connection would deter them but it does leave a little Greek enclave on the alien coast.

The central feature of the port is the stone jetty built to accommodate the coasters which originally transported emery. This was fed by the aerial ropeway which disgorged its mineral contents into a large terminal centrally placed in the little settlement. The buckets fed the emery into trains of small steel trucks which, in turn, were hauled out to the jetty.

Today the emery terminal is a fascinating piece of industrial archaeology in the making. The ropeway gantries are partly dismembered but the railway lines and the trucks are still in position. Even the tiny turntable which redirected the trucks singly towards the jetty is emplaced on the lines. The reason for the very existence of the system, the mineral emery still fills the trucks. Large chunks of glittering, dense, steel grey rock are present everywhere, recovered from the earth but now unwanted.

The trucks are red with rust. Bright green weeds are now shooting up in the deserted marshalling yard. A row of trucks even lies along the edge of the beach, used by the locals as a protection from the wind. Though the heart of Moutsouna has effectively stopped beating, the cadaver seems unaware of the problem and the shouting children and the laughing parents ignore the misfortune. However, what may be of considerable interest to the geologist or industrial archaeologist can only be a blot on the tourist landscape.

The jetty today is of interest only to a few local fishermen. Adjacent to it, at the northern end of the bay, is a taverna with tamarisk trees and pleasant shade. Small fish, just pulled out of the sea, are served there with chips, retsina and the inevitable *psomi* (bread). The consumption of these is so enjoyable that the long trek to reach the site is forgotten and fortitude is gained for the even more taxing return journey.

The climb out of Moutsouna is fairly steep and the road is rough in places. One thing is certain and that is that the short cuts across the hairpins which were so inviting when looking down on them, have lost their appeal on the return ascent. A jumble of rocks and no visible outlet generally ensure that the more circuitous route is followed.

Again, the possibility of hitching a lift is remote but there is always something to be learned. An old and noisy shepherd, heard whistling across the hillside, appears on the road ahead and gets involved in conversation. He is from Apiranthos. A car is grinding noisily up the hill behind and he gives a knowing wink. He does not really thumb the car but stands in the middle of the road with his arms, and stick, widespread. Great! He has secured a lift! How genuinely kind these Greek country people are. He pokes his head through the car window for a few words in his gruff voice. The door is opened, in he leaps and waves goodbye as he speeds on to Apiranthos.

Lionas

An alternative route to the east coast lies midway between Moutsouna and Apollona. It leads off the main north road just before the village of Koronos, a strip of newly engineered tarmac.

The first section descends a steep-sided gorge. Massive cliffs, banded pink and white in some places and grey and white in others, line the sides. Bristling pads of purple flowers add a splash of contrasting colour but it does not do to let the attention stray too far from the road. Mounds of dark emery are stacked on its surface at intervals like an impromptu chicane to trap the unwary speedster. A few are whitewashed as an afterthought, perhaps in response to some unfortunate's demise.

Closer inspection of the rock walls shows that the marble is laced with black emery veins, pockets and spots sparkling with flakes of mica. A maze of cave-like interconnected workings thread their way through the outcrops. Some descend sharply to lower levels and are surmounted by steel platforms and decaying winding mechanisms. Overhead, emery laden buckets swing forlornly on the rusting aerial ropeway. It is like a *Marie Celeste* of mining, the workforce having abandoned the enterprise in mid-stroke.

The road snakes down the narrow valley until it opens out into the green vale at the head of the Bay of Lionas. It terminates abruptly in the dust behind the beach alongside the ubiquitous stacks of emery. The solitary bus of the day parks here after leaving Naxos at noon and awaits its return journey at 6 pm.

The beach is open to north east winds which propel pounding breakers on to the shore. This lashing over the centuries has ground the rocks down to spheres and discs of white marble and black hornfels. Bathing proves to be a little hard on the feet and the waves suit only a handful of boisterous and masochistic Greeks. Other families, more sedately, lie in the shade of the few fishing boats drawn high up on to the shore.

A handful of old cottages occupy the south side of the bay, wedged in against the steep valley side. To the north more newly built apartments lie on a more gentle slope. A path curves round the side of the bay below them and above the low cliffs of this marble shore. A little tree provides a shady perch for those in contemplative mood and a relatively short walk exchanges a wild coastline for holiday homes.

Two small tavernas are found in Lionas. One, the **Riaca,** is beneath the green trees of the valley floor where the road enters the hamlet. The other, the **Adonis,** has a little raised terrace above the end of the road and a view out to the bay. The range of food on offer is not great but if *marides,* the little fish caught locally, and Greek salad satisfy at midday then it can be very pleasant. The local wine, translucent rather than transparent, and having a curiously scented sweet flavour, will definitely not appeal to all. However, a quarter of a litre lubricates the ambience. It is always a surprise and a delight when the proprietor emerges with a large plate of ice cold water melon to express his pleasure at your company.

Accommodation

Hotels on Naxos

Class	Name	Location	Beds	Tel. (code 0285)
B	Aneza	Naxos	12	—
B	Ariadne	Naxos	46	22452
B	Glaros	Naxos	14	—
C	Acroyali	Naxos	27	22922
C	Aegeon	Naxos	40	22852
C	Anessi	Naxos	25	22758
C	Apollon	Naxos	34	22468
C	Barbouni	Naxos	26	22535
C	Coronis	Naxos	60	22626
C	Grotta	Naxos	35	22646
C	Helmos	Naxos	21	22455
C	Hermes	Naxos	32	22220
C	Iliovassilema	Naxos	39	22107
C	Kymata	Naxos	26	22438
C	Naxos Beach	Naxos	50	22928
C	Nissaki	Naxos	30	22876
C	Panorama	Naxos	33	22330
C	Renetta	Naxos	23	22952
C	Sergis	Naxos	85	22355
C	Zeus	Naxos	29	22912

In Naxos town there are many D and E category hotels and rooms to let. Some of the latter are in houses within the Chora, the old centre of the town, but others are in more modern blocks on the southern St George's Bay margin of the built up area.

Eating out

Outside Naxos town there is little choice among eating places. Beaches have one or two tavernas, closed out of season and offering a very limited menu when they are open. The more remote from Naxos town, the more sparsely distributed are the beach taverna though there is a small choice in Apollona and Moutsouna. The character of some of the town restaurants is noted below.

Kali Kardia An old fashioned, white fronted restaurant in the middle of the waterfront with tables on the pavement and on the

Waterfront restaurant in Naxos, the Kali Kardia.

harbour edge over the road. Traditional Greek menu with recommended *souvlakia* and red mullet grilled with lemon.

Manolis Garden Restaurant In the heart of the twisting ways of the Chora. A little verdant courtyard within enclosing buildings. Reasonably priced traditional dishes but crowded and prone to run out of items later in the evening.

Thomas Grill Located in a cul-de-sac close to the O.T.E. at the south end of the harbour. Excellent charcoal grilled food but the best buy is the shish-kebab sliced off a vertical electric grill. Order everything at the outset as second orders rarely materialise.

O Tsitas Located on the narrow shopping street parallel to the waterfront. In the heart of the town and justifiably popular. Serves typical Greek dishes with large 'chips' and a *horiatiki* salad thick with feta cheese. Small squid can be recommended especially accompanied by Kourtaki retsina. Go late and the menu rapidly shrinks.

Pitzaria Next door to O Tsitas and equally busy. Its range is not limited to pizzas but includes many commendable Greek dishes.

Christos Charcoal grill at the northern end of the town a few yards from the harbour front. Tables fill the narrow street of this genuine *psistaria*. Has a limited menu but highly recommended liver, *souvlakia* and red snapper.

Nikos A high class restaurant extending from the waterfront balconies over the Commercial Bank through a large indoor area to street tables extending up the terraces behind the building. This offers the widest possible range of foods displayed in closed cabinets. Outside, the charcoal grill attracts the passer-by to an impressive array of lobsters, mullet, snappers and the most enormous groupers.

To Kastro In the municipal park high on the slopes of the Kastro with its tables around the bust of the Macedonian Wars' fighter, Christos Pradounas. Bats flit by as the sun sets over the scene. Really excellent beef and vegetable casserole with a cheese crust.

Vassilis Taverna Just a short distance from the central square up Odos Agios Nikodimou. Well advertised and brightly lit with much on offer but little available for late comers.

Lucullus Across Nikodimou from Vassilis, this is a tiny taverna with plastic covered tables inside. There is not much on show but good Greek grilled food is served and it is inevitably crowded.

Bakaliarakia High on the Chora, the Bakaliarakia has a cane and vine covered enclosure decorated by coloured gourds and a charcoal grill. Two overworked, but very efficient men provide the service of reasonably priced snappers, chicken and *souvlakia*.

Kazanakia Located on the main road out of Naxos. This is a cane-framed restaurant with bouzouki music. The service is quick and pleasant. Dishes include green beans in tomato, liver and squid served with locally produced Vareli wine.

O Koutouki A very narrow alley, Odos Persephonis, a little way into the Chora is the attractive setting of the O Koutouki taverna. Tables fill the flags but cater for only a few people.

Apolafsis A traditional Greek taverna with a large range of dishes. The Apolafsis is crowded nightly, at least in part because its balcony overlooks the harbour and the sun setting over Paros.

In addition to the restaurants and grills in town, there are two other areas which possess a variety of amenities. One is the main hotel and apartment region south of the Chora along the roads to Agios Prokopios and Agios Giorgios. The other is the line of tavernas and bars along Agios Giorgios beach. In the former, along Agiou Arseniou, is the video-disco bar of **Papagallo,** the pink and noisy **Medusa** bar, the **Eravi** bar, the **Nisiotopoula** or 'Island Girl' grill and the **Village** breakfast and coffee bar. Perhaps one of the most pleasant is the *kafe-zacharoplasteion* of **O Panagiotis.** Agios Giorgios is really for those who like their nights to be boisterous and noisy. The **Kavouri** is a conventional restaurant but there is a string of night club discos, the **Asterias, Rainbow** and **Paradise.** One of the most interesting is the **Flisvos** with its tiny mill tower on the edge of the sand overlooking the wind surfers and serving its own varieties of yoghurt.

Naxian octopi awaiting the grill while dehydrating in the sun.

Vessel	Monday	Tuesday	Wednesday	Thursday	Friday	Saturday	Sunday
Naxos		Paros Piraeus (d.21.30)	Paros Piraeus (d.21.30)	Paros Piraeus (d.21.30)	Paros Piraeus (d.21.30)	Paros Piraeus (d.21.30)	Paros Piraeus (d.21.30)
Lemnos	Paros Piraeus (d.11.00)		Ios Santorini Heraklion (d.14.30)	Paros Piraeus (d.11.00)	Ios Sikinos Folegandros Santorini Heraklion (d.15.00)	Paros Syros Piraeus (d.13.00)	Ios Santorini Heraklion (d.14.30)
Giorgios Express			Ios Santorini (d.14.30) / Paros Piraeus (d.22.30)	Ios Santorini (d.14.30) / Paros Piraeus (d.22.30)		Paros Piraeus (d.11.30)	Ios Santorini (d.00.20) / Paros Piraeus (d.11.30)
Nissos Chios		Paros Piraeus (d.09.30)			Paros Piraeus (d.09.30)		

Vessel	Monday	Tuesday	Wednesday	Thursday	Friday	Saturday	Sunday
Atlas II		Paros Syros Rafina (d.17.00)		Paros Syros Rafina (d.17.00)			
Santorini		Ios Sikinos Folegandros Santorini (d.16.30)	Paros Syros Piraeus (d.12.30)				
Nereus						Amorgos Astypalea (d.24.00)	Paros Syros Piraeus (d.21.30)
Miaoulis		Amorgos Astypalea Rhodes (d.02.00)					

Table 14   Ferry services from Naxos in vessels likely to operate in all weathers

Vessel	Monday	Tuesday	Wednesday	Thursday	Friday	Saturday	Sunday
Ios	Mykonos (d.13.15)	Mykonos (d.13.15)	Mykonos (d.13.15)	Mykonos (d.13.15)	Mykonos (d.13.15)	Mykonos (d.13.15)	Mykonos (d.13.15)
Skopelitis	Iraklia Schinoussa Koufonissia Amorgos (d.16.00)	Iraklia Schinoussa Koufonissia Amorgos (d.16.00)	Mykonos (d.12.30) / Iraklia Schinoussa Koufonissia Amorgos (d.16.00)	Iraklia Schinoussa Koufonissia Amorgos (d.14.00)	Iraklia Schinoussa Koufonissia Amorgos (d.16.00)	Mykonos (d.12.30) / Iraklia Schinoussa Koufonissia Amorgos (d.16.00)	Mykonos (d.12.30) / Iraklia Schinoussa Koufonissia Amorgos (d.16.00)
Daphne II		Delos Mykonos Naxos (d.09.00)	Piso Livadi Mykonos Piso Livadi Naxos (d.07.30)	Delos Mykonos Naxos (d.09.00)	Delos Mykonos Naxos (d.09.00)	Santorini (d.17.00)	Delos Mykonos Naxos (d.09.00)

Latsos II		Paros Sifnos (d.09.00)	Paros Sifnos (d.09.00)	Paros Sifnos (d.09.00)	Paros Sifnos (d.09.00)	Paros Sifnos (d.09.00)	Paros Sifnos (d.09.00)

Table 15 Ferry services from Naxos dependent on windy conditions

(These services may not operate during the prolonged and powerful northerly meltemi winds. In some cases winds may cause re-routing: thus the *Latsos II* may call into Piso Livadi in south Paros instead of Paroikia in the north. The M/V *Ios*, coming from Ios is commonly overcrowded when it arrives at Naxos and it may be difficult to obtain tickets to Mykonos. Certainly, it would be unwise to rely on these ships to connect with other ferry or air services as delays of days are not unusual.)

139

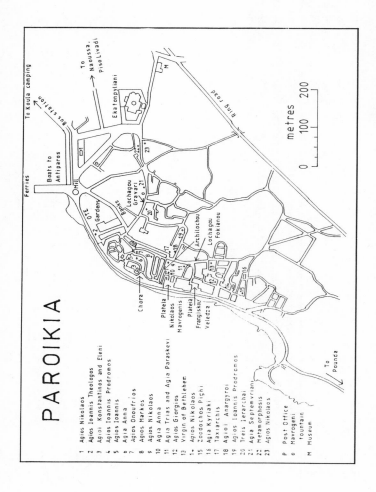

PAROIKIA

1 Agios Nikolaos
2 Agios Ioannis Theologos
3 Agioi Konstantinos and Eleni
4 Agios Ioannis Prodromos
5 Agios Ioannis
6 Agia Anna
7 Agios Onoufrios
8 Agios Markos
9 Agios Nikolaos
10 Agia Anna
11 Agia Trias and Agia Paraskevi
12 Agios Giorgios
13 Virgin of Bethlehem
14 Agios Nikolaos
15 Zoodochos Pighi
16 Agia Kyriaki
17 Taxiarchis
18 Agioi Anargyroi
19 Agios Ioannis Prodromos
20 Treis Ierarchai
21 Agia Septemvriani
22 Metamorphosis
23 Agios Nikolaos

P Post Office
o Mavrogeni fountain
M Museum

ELEVEN

Paros

Paros, or its port Paroikia, is approximately seven hours sail from Piraeus or a little over an hour from Naxos. It has a recently constructed small airport near Alyki in the southwest where the Germans developed a wartime airstrip. Improving external and internal connections spell change. Paros has seen more progress — if change is progress — than Naxos but it still remains a very typical Cycladic Island. It may be, of course, that the benefits of tourism, which has stemmed the exodus of population and the decline of property, will be outweighed by the total annihilation of Cycladic culture and way of life. It is impossible to attain a balance where development is held in check and *romiosini* (Greekness) is retained. The island Greeks need a new economic injection which probably only tourism can provide. If this means prosperity then it is more desirable than poverty and discomfort allied to tradition.

By comparison with Naxos, Paros has a gentler landscape. There are broad areas of low relief and the hills appear more rounded, open and less furrowed than their Naxian counterparts. The sun shines out of a pale sky on to smooth yellowed slopes speckled with white box-like dwellings and patched by chequered villages.

The coastal settlements are tucked away, hidden from the open sea by projecting headlands and rocky islets. Each is revealed begrudgingly to the incoming steamer as it cleaves its way into the sheltered bay.

Paroikia

The principal town, called both Paros and Paroikia, is protected from the north by the long scalloped headland of Akrotiri Agios Fokas and by the steep-walled granite islets which guard the

141

Paroikia: Cycladic terrace on the kastro of Agioi Konstantinos and Eleni.

entrance to the bay. Paroikia spreads itself along the low shores of the bay for over a mile and its outskirts rest on the lower slopes of the hills of Latomia Marmarou to the east.

Paroikia, too, has its proliferation of attractive little chapels and, unlike many on Mykonos and Naxos, these are visible and accessible without effort. Several that visitors to Paroikia are most likely to come across are identified on the town plan (p.143).

The Kastro

The central feature of many Greek island towns is a site set high in a conical hill and known as a Chora. In some cases the hill has been defensively based and is called the Kastro. It may be detached from the port or growth may merge the two as at Naxos. The Kastro at Paroikia lies immediately beside the waterfront in the town centre and occupies a raised mound rather than an impregnable hill. Nevertheless its pedigree is undisputed as it incorporates the foundations of the Classical Temples of Apollo and Demeter, the castle of the Venetians from the early Middle Ages and the seventeenth century church of Agioi Konstantinos and Eleni.

The **Kastro** is the nucleus of Paroikia and it is charming. Certainly it shows the ravages of time as one generation of occupants after another has vandalised or utilised the products of the labour of its predecessors. Where today such actions cause disharmony at best and an eyesore at worst, here in Paroikia white marble, whitewash and time have blended the periods into one. The creations of one era simply grow out of another and merge with it. Fortunately, too, the trappings of the twentieth century are not much in evidence in this part of town.

On the seaward side the Kastro is terraced by stone walls over which plants trail in a miniature 'hanging gardens' of Paroikia. Stone steps scale the hill on either side of these terraces. To landward the Kastro is defined by the remains of the **Venetian castle** wall constructed from 1207 by Marco Sanoudo, the first tenant of the Duchy of the Archipelago of the Cyclades. The construction of this fortress was achieved at the expense of the temples built at about 600 BC on the summit of the hill. These were demolished and their dressed blocks and cylindrical columns of white marble were reconstituted into the jigsaw of the walls.

Scant traces of the **Temples of Apollo and Demeter** remain visible on the hill top. Instead the church of **Agioi Konstantinos and Eleni** provides a beautiful replacement. Under its blue dome, the western gable is stepped and surmounted by a belfry with a serrated arch. Its gable wall is inset with a radially pierced stone light above the

143

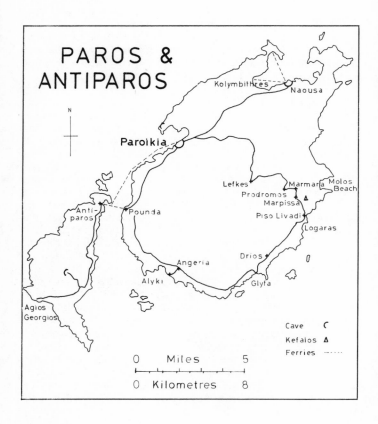

PAROS & ANTIPAROS

N

Kolymbithres — Naousa

Paroikia

Lefkes — Marmara — Molos Beach
Prodromos
Marpissa △
Piso Livadi
Anti-
paros
Pounda
Logaras

Agios
Georgios

Angeria
Alyki
Drios

Glyfa

Cave ⊂
Kefalos △
Ferries ------

| 0 | Miles | 5 |

| 0 | Kilometres | 8 |

Doorway of Agios Konstantinos in Paroikia.

remains of a blue ceramic tile cross. Beneath these is a gem of a doorway in which the marble frame is carved into an intricate tracery of flowers and leaves. Built on to the side of the chapel is a terrace shaded by a beautiful triple arched vault set on slender pillars and enhanced by oleander bushes. The summit of the Kastro could well be regarded as its crowning glory.

The little lanes that curl around the citadel walls are without the shops and cafés of the rest of Paroikia. They are tiny white canyons walled by Cycladic architecture. A crowning church does not preclude others. Two of them. **Agios Ioannis** and **Agios Ioannis Prodromos** (St John the Baptist) stand side by side at the northeastern end of the Kastro. Their simple belfries and doors overlook the white cement net which laces the flagged way up the hill. Another tiny chapel, **Agia Anna,** is built into the outside of the Venetian wall. Its plain white vault is set in a plethora of temple blocks and columnals encased in climbing pelargoniums.

The north side of the town

Outside the Kastro, the meeting place of Paroikia is the waterfront **windmill** at the base of the ferry jetty. This houses the Touristiki Astinomia, the Tourist Police, who give arrivals advice on accommodation and transport. It usually has visitors perched on the wall around it and is swathed in a variety of backpacks. Where else in the world could one leave a bag unattended all day and expect to find it intact?

On the north side of the mill and two hundred metres from it, the waterfront forms the island's bus terminal and then leads into the first bay and its camp site at Livadia. Between the mill and the buses is the blue domed and brilliant white chapel of **Agios Nikolaos,** free standing on the pavement in gorgeous isolation. Adjacent to it is a small triangular-shaped piece of parkland with pine trees inclined steeply away from the pressures of the *meltemi*. Roads on either side of this green belt lead to the high school and to one of the most famous of Paroikian buldings, the **Church of Ekatonpyliani.**

Ekatonpyliani is vast by comparison with the host of white chapels. It is also one of the oldest in Greece having been constructed under the rule of Justinian in the latter part of the sixth century. The Emperor directed Isidore, architect of St Sophia, to undertake the work and he, in turn, delegated the task to his Parian apprentice, Ignatius. The Byzantine edifice, however, has been reconstructed from time to time largely as a result of the ravages of earthquakes in the tenth century, 1507, 1773 and 1783. Raids

Sponge fishing boat visiting Paroikia harbour from Kalymnos.

by Arabs and by pirates over a very long period of time have also taken their toll.

The name of the great church is open to some debate. If it is Ekatonpyliani then it would appear to be the church of a hundred doors as *ekaton* means one hundred and *pyli* means gateway. However, it may, more correctly, be Katapoliana meaning below or 'within the town'; Katapola is a very common Cycladic place name. The church is dedicated to *Panagia,* the Virgin Mary, whose silver encased icon is carried around the town by a naval escort on that busiest of festive days, 15 August. The church also houses the relics of Agia Theoktisti around whose life a colourful local legend has grown. Her remains, too, are paraded in procession on 9 November.

The most unfortunate aspect of Ekatonpyliani is the way that it is screened from view. Reconstruction programmes at various periods until recent times have created an attractive piece of Byzantine stone and tile work but most of it is surrounded by plain two-storey monastic domestic building which totally obscures the church. The rest of the building nestles shyly behind stone walls and cypresses. Only the nearby high school grounds gain even a moderate picture of the church.

One hundred metres beyond the church is the **Archaeological Museum.** Most such regional collections have been limited by the requirements of the National Museum in Athens. This means that collections are of lesser works and those of specific local interest. In Paroikia, the premier exhibit is a fragment of the Parian Chronicle which, along with a lot of other material, had been used in the building of the Venetian walls. The Chronicle was carved in white marble in 264 BC as a chronological catalogue of the births and deaths of outstanding literary figures and related cultural events. It is written in the Attic dialect and covers 93 lines. The major part was discovered in 1627 and is now housed in the Ashmolean, Oxford while the Paroikian fragment was located in 1897. Other items of some interest include a mosaic of Herakles, winged victories, ancient *kouroi* (statues), bas-reliefs and, in the museum courtyard, a marble plaque, discovered in 1949 and inscribed with a biography of the Parian warrior poet Archilochus. An Ionic capital has also been later inscribed and used as a burial for Archilochus and this, too, is in the museum.

Central Paroikia

The waterfront windmill not only has roads radiating from it leading along the coast in either direction and southeast to Ekatonpyliani but also southwest into the commercial heart of

Paroikia. This route has cafés, gardens and offices grouped around it near the mill in as regular a pattern as Paroikia can muster, but it then dives into narrow paved pedestrian ways with arches and the white cubic buildings found throughout the Cyclades. Here and there simple but asymmetrical Cycladic patterns are broken by the more formal designs of Venetian architecture, a residue of protracted Venetian influence both during and after their period of administration. The same influence is still seen in the retention of Venetian family names such as Venieri and Crispi.

Another tangible reminder of Paroikian roots takes the form of three marble wall fountains, two of them on the main street of the town, Lochagou Fokianou, and the third between the Kastro and Ekatonpyliani on Lochagou Gravari. These are inscribed with the date of their construction, 1777, and the name of their donor, Nikolaos Mavrogenis. The latter was a Parian who, during the period of Ottoman rule, rose to power in Constantinople, becoming governor of Moldavia. The niece of Nikolaos, Manto Mavrogenis, is also commemorated by a central statue for her leading role in the War of Independence from the Ottomans.

Paroikia is a charming introduction to Paros in spite of the bustle of its waterfront and the neverending stream of ferried visitors. Nothing is more striking along its quiet ways than the greenery which breaks up the all pervading white, from the tamarisks of Livadia beach to the bougainvillea draped across the arches and walls of the town. The Parians have an innate artistry, a floral flair to complement the cubism of the architecture.

Naoussa and the north

From the head of Paroikia Bay at Livadia to Ormos Plastira, the equivalent position on Naoussa Bay, there is a broad vale separating low ridges to the northwest from the central Parian mountains. A good tarmac road with gentle gradients follows the vale, linking Paroikia to Naoussa, a distance of 11 kilometres.

Apart from the bays at either end of the route, the area to the northwest has a steep, rocky and inaccessible coast which is very open to the ravages of the *meltemi*. The ridge reaches a height of only 200 metres and its slopes are gentle. The area houses a number of classical and ecclesiastical sites but successive generations have pillaged the earlier sites so that little is to be seen and the remains are for archaeological devotees intent on making a comprehensive survey of every block.

Naousa harbour crowded with fishing boats.

At the southern end of the ridge is **Akrotiri Agios Fokas** with its scalloped south-facing bays. These have sandy beaches accessible by tramping round from Paroikia or by the small boats plying across the bay from the jetty. These beaches are narrow, busy and not for the visitor requiring seclusion or scenic settings.

Northward from the bays and on the seaward side of Akrotiri Agios Fokas is **Archilochos Cave,** set high in the steep cliffs. This is the supposed location of the classical poet's refuge for contemplation. Better substantiated remains, but rather less substantial, are the classical sites of the **Delion** and the **Sanctuary of Aphrodite.** The former is attained by a climb on to the ridge by a path from the Bay of Livadia. Only some foundation stones remain but the site, formerly housing the Sanctuary of the Apollo of Delos, offers views in clear conditions to the island of Delos itself.

Even less is to be seen of the **Sanctuary of Aphrodite** on the slopes of Kounadhos hill and nothing at all of the temples which once occupied its summit. The demise of these structures does not indicate failings on the part of the designers but the needs of the local farmhouses, town dwellings, lime makers and later ecclesiastical buildings. In fact much went into the construction of a Byzantine basilica at **Treis Ekklesies,** just outside Paroikia by the Naoussa-Lefkes road junction. Other materials came from the now erased monument of the Heroon of Archilochos. This has gone the way of the others leaving enigmatic remains.

Monasteries lie on either side of the vale to Naoussa. On the western side is the small and now defunct establishment of **Agios Michail Taxiarchis** dating from 1609. Opposite to it, in a small valley dissecting the central uplands, is wedged the large and flourishing **Moni Longovardas,** housing an agricultural community with interests in wine making, baking, book binding and icon painting. As with many monasteries female visitors are not welcomed. The external appearance is of a vast white rectangular prison block, uncompromising and forbidding. Inside its courtyard the view mellows around the tall cypresses, storeys of arched windows and the silver-domed chapel with twin belfry.

Naoussa and its bay

As the main road approaches Naoussa, apartments and hotels in various states of readiness cloak the eastern shores of **Ormos Plastira.** Sandy beaches below them provide the attraction but a good deal of tourist debris litters them in spite of the fervent pleas of the Naoussa council. In fact Naoussa has set out in no uncertain

Reflections on a fishing boat at Naousa.

terms in distributed literature its rules for tourists. Many are just common sense ordinances but included are the banning of camping on beaches, drug taking, nudism and topless bathing except at Monasteri. Litter is to be placed in receptacles or to be removed if none is available. Noise of all types is to be kept at low levels and respect for the local siesta is also regarded as important.

The road crosses a bridge over the dry bed of a river and turns right into the eucalyptus-shaded square of **Naoussa.** The spreading branches provide a haven for those waiting for the hourly buses to Paroikia or seeking a shady respite and a cooling drink in the heat of the day.

The square is a pleasant and bustling centre but the town is also focused upon its beautiful harbour. The **Kastro** of Naoussa was constructed tightly around the port and a small Venetian round tower was built at the end of a breakwater protecting its entrance. The charm of the harbour lies partly in its size. If small is beautiful then this is a gem. It is not only small, rectangular and almost enclosed but is absolutely crammed with caiques. Not even motor ferries or yachts spoil the uniquely Greek character of its gently swaying fleet, dappled by the sun reflected off the water. Caiques with their arched decks and curved prows and timbers painted in whites and blues and reds are evocative of all that is Greece. It's a bit sad to see amid the *Agios Constantinos* and similar saintly names inscribed in the bows, one discordantly named *Kiss Me.*

Naoussa harbour is a working place. Its vessels are fishing boats. The quays are strewn with nets as well as lashed by spray when the *meltemi* drives waves against the windward breakwater. The fruits of the work are evident in the whitewashed restaurants which surround it. Some are large and offer delectable *barbouni* or red mullet while others offer charcoal grilled *octopodi* with an ouzo to those with more acclimatised Greek palates.

The town, like other Venetian settlements, appears to be a shapeless maze of narrow paved roads criss-crossed by archways and gates. Fewer domestic dwellings display the artistry and whitewash of the tourist-conscious Cyclades. Likewise shops are fewer and less garishly oriented to the tourist market. Naoussa presents the appearance of being a real community which does not simply live for the summer influx. Its apparently disordered layout is not totally without plan. The road system is based upon a design of concentric ways focused upon the harbour. However, the best laid plans are apt to go astray when rebuilding over centuries diverts the building line from the preconceived notion.

Following the road east out of Naoussa, within the sheltered confines of Naoussa Bay, initially means a short steep climb past the church, windmill and tourist arpartments and then a drop to the low, undulating and fretted coast beyond. Beaches tend to be stony, the road dusty and the rocky landscape is covered with a low spiny vegetation with junipers prevailing in the lower and sandier areas. Pocket-sized beaches are wedged and formed between the rocks before the persistent wind drifts the grains up the gentle slopes around the junipers. The northeast corner of Paros at **Akrotiri Agia Maria** is a quiet and lonely place but **Ambelas,** just to the south, has a beach, a taverna and a relatively good and short road connection to Naoussa.

One of the most pleasant features of the Naoussa area is the ferries which regularly ply between the outer harbour of the town and the more distant shores of Naoussa Bay. The bay is nearly 5½ km at its widest point but it has an entrance of only 2 km. Naoussa is nearly centrally placed relative to the mouth of the bay and is, therefore, susceptible to the prevailing northerlies but the flanks of the bay are much more sheltered.

Some boats may run to **Platis Ammos,** a broader beach on the northeast headland but one that is exposed to the elements. The two most regular and popular services run to **Kolymbithres** and to the **Monasteri** beach both of which lie in the lea of the western headlands of Akrotiri Korax and Akrotiri Tourkos. At both of these sites the waters are calm but the small vessels need the power and cover they possess when they run broadside to the waves across the open water from Naoussa.

Kolymbithres

Kolymbithres can, in fact, also be approached on foot by a track branching off the Paroikia road around Plastira Bay. It is a marvellous place. Local literature would have you believe that it is a wonder of the world inadvertently omitted from standard lists but it is not that. Its attraction lies in the granite which forms the ridge that sweeps down into the bay in a jumble of outcrops and boulders. In many places on Paros the granites are layered and cleaved but these are massive. Their character here is imposed by the pattern of joints which have developed in the rock and by the effects of marine weathering on its minerals.

Jointing in granites commonly follows two or three axes or planes. One of these is parallel to the surface of the original intrusion and may result either from the contraction of the cooling rock or from its expansion after cooling as the weight of overlying material is removed by erosion. The result is the formation of a

Kolymbithres: granite all at sea.

Kolymbithres: weathered granite mushroom.

series of thick concentric shells which are fractured by other joints at right angles to them. The latter have been caused by tensions set up through folding and expansion.

The joints have been selectively eroded by the salt water leaving the rock furrowed, ribbed and undercut into mushroom and roofed forms. The lower parts of the rock, which are most subject to the sea's attack, are pale grey from a distance or speckled on close viewing where dark mica and grey quartz fleck the white feldspar. However, the upper surfaces have an ochreous stain, forming a sharply defined roof. This has probably been precipitated over the original granite surface having been leached from the overlying soils as limonite, an iron oxide.

Here and there the granite has been selectively weathered and etched to form most attractive honeycomb tracery, especially when the sunlight penetrates the recesses to create patterns of light and shade.

One of the most pleasant features of Kolymbithres is the lucid blue waters based on the pale sands which underlie them. Even in stormy weather these are transparent and clear, lapping on the granite rocks. Small pockets of sandy beach fill the interstices between the outcrops for swimmers and picnickers, though there is a more extensive sandy beach stretching around Plastira Bay towards Naoussa. Tucked away behind the rocks there is a taverna to make it unnecessary to cart masses of liquid refreshment to this idyllic spot.

Monasteri

It is possible to hike from Kolymbithres to the second ferry terminal on the west of Naoussa Bay, Monasteri Beach. Indeed, probably the best way to see this area is to visit Kolymbithres, walk to Monasteri and then return to Naoussa via the second ferry. The walk is along low earth cliffs with stony beaches and small curves of sand just a few feet below.

After about a mile the little path opens out on to the beach where there is a boatyard with caiques propped up in various states of repair. The boats are no less appealing out of the water than in and they also have the benefit of the monastery of **Agios Ioannis Prodromos** as a backdrop. As elsewhere, the site for the monastery was chosen for its suitability for undisturbed contemplation, as well as with an eye for the beautiful, and it gives the impression of growing out of the rounded granite of a headland projecting into the bay.

On one side of the monastery is the boatyard and on the other

Shipyard by the monastery of Ioannis Prodromos.

a small sandy cove in the lea of the entrance headland of **Akrotiri Tourkos.** The blue-domed monastery over years has looked down on the waters of the deserted cove. The monastery is now without devotees in residence and perhaps it is just as well as they could not now give undivided attention to their devotions. The sandy cove is known as Monasteri Beach and it, together with the smoother granite slabs around it, is the objective of the boatloads of sunworshippers that disembark hourly at the small jetty. Notices advise the visitors to refrain from disrobing within the bounds of the monastery grounds but some of the smoothest rocks are on its headland below its walls. Golden brown glowing bodies are all around and clothes of any type are not much in evidence. The monastery is set in a world of Adam and Eve.

From Paroikia to:	
Naoussa	8.0,9.0,9.15,9.30,10.0,10.30,11.0, 11.15,11.30,12.00,12.30,1.0,2.0,2.30, 3.0,4.0,4.30,5.0,5.15,6.0,6.30,7.0, 8.0,9.0.
Ambelas	9.30,11.0,2.30,5.15
Pounda	8.0,10.0,12.0,2.0,4.0,7.0
Alyki-Angeria	7.0,9.0,10.0,11.0,12.0,1.0,2.0, 3.0,4.0,5.0,6.0,8.0
Lefkes-Drios	8.0,9.0,9.15,10.0,10.30,11.0 12.0,12.30,1.0,2.0,2.30,3.0 4.0,4.30,5.0,6.0,7.0,8.0,9.0
From Naoussa to:	
Drios	9.30,11.30,3.15,4.45

Table 16   Bus services on Paros

Central Paros

Paros has a broad elliptical shape. It is both at its widest and its highest in the centre where it reaches 755 metres at Mt Profitis Elias. This is comparable with the English Pennines and, like those mountains, is a rounded upland with low vegetation and relatively few rocky outcrops. Its summit, although capped with the inevitable chapels, Agioi Pandes and Agios Profitis Elias, is spoiled as a spectacle by the huge red and white aerials of a communications complex.

The thickened waist of Paros is traversed by a tarmac road and an hourly bus service from Paroikia. This route zig-zags its way across the spurs and valleys of the highland, a distance of a little over 15 kilometres but one which provides an essential service linking a chain of upland villages, giving them access to the sophisticated amenities of Paroikia. The same route affords the visitor an opportunity to experience the charm of these still unspoiled settlements as well as leading to the southeast coast resorts of Piso Livadi, Logaras, Chrisi Akti and Drios.

Marathi

The road follows the southern side of the valley opening out at Livadia beside Paroikia. It gradually climbs to the head of the valley and on to the island's watershed at Marathi, 4 kilometres away. Current works taking place to improve the road have moved earth and rock and left the underlying character of this site exposed. Marathi is built on marble, one of the most famous sources in the ancient world and still used in the mid-19th century to provide some of the material for Napoleon's tomb.

The modern fresh exposures demonstrate the nature and merit of the Parian marble but a little off the road there are ancient shafts leading some 100 metres into subterranean marble workings. Within the central shaft there is a bas-relief and inscription, possibly attributable to the Classical Period of development when this marble was used for the sculpting of the Venus de Milo. The reason for the widespread acclaim of Parian marble lies in its purity. Marble is limestone which has been subjected to temperatures of up to 700°C that have recrystallised the calcium carbonate into a granular, sparkling sugary texture. Limestones themselves contain a variety of mineral impurities which impart colour to the subsequent marble. Only pure limestones produce a translucent white and unblemished marble such as that of Paros.

Also accessible to the Marathi marble quarries is the monastery of **Agios Minas** with its strong buttressed walls which lies in the valley behind Marathi and only a short walk away.

Lefkes

The main road passes through a singularly green area by the standards of Paros beyond Marathi. Olive trees are plentiful close to the little village of **Kostos** in the valley below. At nine kilometres from Paroikia is one of the largest villages, **Lefkes,** though like Marathi this has declined with the demise of the marble workings and the subsequent loss of employment. Its former glory also lay in its administrative significance under Ottoman rule as well as its relative safety during piratical attacks upon coastal settlements.

Historical significance apart, Lefkes enjoys a most pleasant site around a valley head where the sheltering ridge is surmounted by windmills and the slopes are clad in a patchwork of olives, pines and cypress. The incline causes the white box-like dwellings to be stacked above one other but interspersed with oleander, cypress and figs. The large mid-19th century church of **Agia Triada** towards the lower part of the town has twin pierced belfry towers capped by tracery crowns projecting above all.

Even rural Greek villages these days have their unspoiled image blemished by a rash of wooden posts, power and telephone lines but Lefkes is still slumbering. Its association with the marble workings means that this stone is copiously used, not least as the paving for its tortuous narrow streets. It has character built in because of its sloping site. There are wells, wheel windows and wooden doorways and, typical of this area, the wedding-cake tier structures seen in many of the chapel belfries. The plethora of Orthodox chapels produces a confusion of saintly names, interior icons and iconostasis (screens). No matter how enthusiastic the student this surfeit causes even these treasures to pall but the external charm is eternal. No two are identical in form and, under varying light conditions, they are delicate and enchanting.

It is downhill from Lefkes either trundling in the usually grossly overcrowded bus or walking. The latter offers an alternative route for, running parallel to the modern road, there is an old paved Byzantine way, generally below the present route, quiet and most pleasant. At about 3½ kilometres there is the little white hamlet of **Prodromos** in which is the church of **Agios Ioannis o Prodromos** (Saint John the Baptist). This Cycladic settlement is still enclosed by a rectilinear wall pierced by a gateway on its eastern side. It lies close by similar villages at **Marmara** and **Marpissa.** All lie within easy walking distance of each other and the fortified hill of **Kefalos.**

Marpissa: street of Arches.

All are worth close inspection.

Marmara means marble. The implication may be a settlement in which this stone is widely used in building but, in fact, whitewash and reconstruction obscure its former significance. The most evident items are the segments of marble columns near the seaward edge of the hamlet. The centres of these have been hollowed out and worn smooth through ages of use for washing and mixing whitewash.

The little lane that leads out of Marmara down to the wide sandy bay of **Ormos Kefalos** (also known as **Molos** beach — see page 140), passes close by these ancient relics but it also gives access to two beautiful little churches. The first encountered has a biscuit coloured tiered belfry of limestone above a small decorative arch of the same material. These contrast with and complement the whitewashed walls of the church. A few yards further on is the unique 17th-century church of **Pera Panagia,** jutting into the flat irrigated fields of tomatoes and melons. The early morning light, streaming in across these fields, illuminates the curious apsidal ends of the double vaulted body of the church, crisp and white against the little copse of trees which shade its western entrance. A tall white-tiered belfry rises above the stepped western gable spanning the two vaults and nestles under the shade of the taller trees. Pera Panagia is not only Cycladic architecture at its most alluring but it has not been hidden by the growth of the village.

Marpissa

The main road out of Marmara climbs up to the village of **Marpissa.** This stands on the watershed of a spur projecting from the central uplands towards the conical hill of Kefalos on the coast. From this site in the lee of Kefalos, Marpissa looks down on Marmara to the north and to Piso Livadi on the coast to the south. Not far from the road on the crest of the ridge is the large red-tiled cathedral church of **Panagià tis Metamorphosis** set high on an open square. This prominent building is not typical of Marpissa. Everywhere its streets are inclined and narrow, a maze of tortuous ways with every corner revealing a new little treasure. It is one of those places in which the attraction is not a single piece of architecture or a particular view but the surprises and pleasures of its every turn. Near to the cathedral a solitary dwarf twisted pine emerges from the stone and whitewash. Elsewhere, the apses and domes of the little chapels, the stepped streets and the corridors of arches take the eye. Increasingly, places like Marpissa are attracting summer visitors seeking a different way and pace of life

Church doorway in Marpissa.

to that available on the coast.

The bus stops in Marpissa on the hill crest where a little *kafeneion* looks across the road to three rather derelict windmills, side by side. Once again it seems such a pity that the charm of these has not been realised and action taken at least to arrest the process of decay. Repaired, they would be things of beauty but in ruin they are just a suitable hoarding for political advertising.

Kefalos

The lane which runs alongside the mills is directed towards the hill of Kefalos. Past a few farmyards it becomes a stony track as it approaches the outcropping marble foundations of the hill where it divides into two. The way to the summit is the less obvious path to the left. It is fairly steep and sinuous but the way has been paved with irregular lumps of stone which have slithered down the slopes from the summit. It is not a very arduous climb but it is not really made for pointed heels. Nevertheless, those with faint hearts might be encouraged by the sight of heavy, elderly women, dedicated to the Orthodox faith, trailing up the slopes in the wake of a priest.

Kefalos means 'head' and presumably refers to the prominent isolated form of the hill. It not only stands out in the southeastern corner of Paros but is equally visible across the channel from distant Naxos. Kefalos is noted for its physical prominence and for its place in history. It represents a heroic and revered episode in Parian development during the Middle Ages.

Paros had prospered under Venetian rule since 1207 but had suffered from the activities of pirates, both directly and through their using Paros as a base. This incurred the displeasure of the Ottomans who claimed that pirate despoliation of their territory had its source in Paros. Eventually the Ottoman fleet attacked when Paros was under the control of the Duke Bernado Sangredo and his wife, Cecilia Venieri. Led by Khair-ed-din Barbarossa (Redbeard), the Ottomans drove the Venetians back from Paroikia. The Duke of the Cyclades retreated to the fortified hill of Kefalos for a last stand. This rocky crested cone offered greater security than Custer's slight mound on the prairies of Montana but the end was equally inevitable. Defeat in 1537 brought to a conclusion the period of Venetian control and introduced over 250 years of Ottoman rule.

Today, the fragmentary remains of the late 15th century Venetian fortifications are found around the hill but there are also the ruins of churches which pre-date the walls. These are crumbling and overgrown with weeds so that the **Evangelismos tis Theotokou** and the **Agia Flouria** are unrecognisable. Also engulfing the defences and early ecclesiastical foundations is a plantation of pines which covers the upper slopes of the cone below the 16th-century monastery on its summit.

The hilltop is a rock platform, cliffed on the eastern seaward side above a steep and open slope. The cliffs are smooth faced and striped with almost horizontal layers of white and red or ochre material. Examined closely, it is seen to be slightly lustrous or even glassy in places. This capping to the hill is a sheet of rhyolite lava which was thick and viscous, even pasty when it was formed. The markings are flow bands developed as it squeezed slowly forward and the vitreous texture, where it exists, indicates the lava being chilled instantly to a natural glass without the ordered atomic structure common to virtually all rocks.

The object today of those who scale Kefalos is to see the monastery **Agios Antonios** and to obtain the magnificent fully circular panorama. The monastery probably occupies a classical temple site though all that can be seen are the blocks, columns and capitals incorporated into the monastery structure. Even then these have been whitewashed, perhaps to cleanse their association with a mythical deity.

The monastery has twin domes and a complex of stepped walls, all glistening brilliant white on the sunseeking summit. On one side there is a beautiful courtyard shaded by a central tree and decorated by a tiny green pine beside the stone covered well. Overlooking this delightful spot a little terrace beside the former quarters of the monks has a unique fencing of whitewashed classical fragments.

One of the surprises of Agios Antonios is its sheltered calm even when the excesses of the *meltemi* are tearing up the surface of the sea far below. Agios Antonios looks down on the coast of southeast Paros. To the northeast is the deep rectangular bay of Ormos Kefalos with its long sandy strand and projecting rocky headlands. To the south Piso Livadi nestles in one of the sequence of small bays in the lowland coast that fades away into the brilliant Aegean light. Marpissa is seen below as a quilt of white over the golden hillsides of central Paros. Pale slopes bask in the summer sun having been shorn of their tresses of grain. The brightly illuminated landscape falls away to the fretted wave-washed shores of southern Paros, another facet of this Cycladic gem.

Southern Paros

In southern Paros the land slopes fairly gently down from the uplands of Profitis Ilias to the coast. There are exceptions where ridges reach down to the shore and project as headlands, notably on the northern side of Piso Livadi, but in most cases there are low rocky platforms and very small cliffs. The coast is crenulated. The layered granitic rocks bulge seaward between pocket sized bays of white sand.

Piso Livadi

Piso Livadi lies at the base of the hillslope crowned by Marpissa and Agios Antonios. Unusually for Paros and the Cyclades, the lower section of this incline is clad in a small plantation of pines and eucalyptus. As the road emerges from this copse the character of the south coast is revealed as one made for holidaymakers rather than for Greeks.

Piso Livadi has been a fishing village and, up to a point, it still is. Its little stone jetty helps to enclose the bay and accommodate a few fishing boats along with a number of yachts and motor vessels. However, the emphasis has changed from fishing to catering for visitors. Behind the arc of the bay the slopes are clad in small hotels and restaurants and, within the harbour area, virtually every building provides rooms or services for the tourist.

The changes have radically altered the form of Piso Livadi but it has the merit of being a very small place. Its *plateia* or central square lies where the road from Marpissa meets the harbour and swings round to follow the shore of the bay. There visitors and Greeks alike sit on the wall to await the bus returning to Paroikia or the one that follows the beaches around the coast to the terminus at Drios. Small restaurants are grouped around the harbour and extend to the jetty. Those nearest the boats specialise in fish and serve some delightful meals. Above them are rooms looking down on the harbour, a really pleasant place to stay.

People migrate to the beaches during the day on this coast but it is pleasant to return to Piso Livadi square, bathed in the late afternoon sun, to enjoy the warmth with a coffee or ouzo at a *kefeneion* overlooking the harbour. As everywhere in Greece, service and the proprietors are very informal. If a marine gladiator among the tourists returns with a catch it can quickly be arranged for a local restaurant to cook it. Both visitors and Greeks enjoy the moment.

The south coastlands of Paros are extensive and the absence of a through bus service has protected parts from development, leaving little havens for those with the will to seek them out. The low-lying nature of much of this coast means that scenically it cannot be spectacular but, in fact, one of the most attractive elements is close to Piso Livadi itself, accessible but tucked away from immediate observation.

Molos and Marmara beaches

Available communications and the surface road naturally lead travellers westward from Piso Livadi but there is a small track to the northeast following steeper coastal slopes around the base of Kefalos hill. It leads out past the church and some modern apartments above a cliff strewn with builder's debris. The prospect is not rendered more attractive by the fact that the main track fairly evidently terminates in the local rubbish heap in a cliff top site a little further on. However, a secondary path climbs part way up the slopes of Kefalos so that a spur leaves the garbage out of sight and then descends to a small collection of buildings near the corner of **Molos Beach.** These include a couple of cafés beside the wide and remarkably empty sands of Molos.

The bay at Molos is deep and almost rectangular, being enclosed by a pair of hilly and rocky headlands. The beach is fine but its relative quietness can only be attributed to its location away from the bus routes at the end of a little lane from Marmara.

Although Molos has a magnificent stretch of sand, there is another beach just a short distance away which is in a very fine setting and quite unlike others on Paros. From the corner of Molos Beach a little track leaves the bobbing boats and cuts across the base of the headland forming the south side of the bay. It opens out near the middle of what is sometimes called **Marmara Beach,** hemmed in by a rocky point to the north and the monastery capped hill of Kefalos to the south.

Again, its emptiness is remarkable although it is small by comparison with Molos. For half of the day, even in the height of the season, it may be empty though the afternoon can bring in a few visitors. The southern half of the beach is backed by low earth cliffs behind which rises the cone of Kefalos. The north half of the bay has near vertical cliffs of soft sandstone beautifully marked with broad red and green strata. The waves surge up to the cliff base excavating little embayments in its face and filling them with pockets of sand just made for a leisurely day.

Unfortunately there is a blemish in almost every paradise. At Marmara Beach the enclosing, towering cliffs keep out the breeze,

Dovecote at Glyfa.

build up the heat and encourage persistent sand flies. It is, however, so attractive a spot that it is well worth carrying cool drinks, insect repellant creams and an aerosol.

The bay at Marmara is scenically dissimilar to most of those in the Cyclades though in no way is it less attractive. Like the islands themselves, it is small and it is not overcrowded. It lacks amenities but retains its natural beauty.

Logaras to Glyfa

Most of the bays are busy in summer because of the bus service following the coast. Adjacent to Piso Livadi is **Logaras Bay** which has cafés and a large self-service restaurant together with a lot of noise. The sandy beach backed by tamarisks is thronged with visitors. Beyond Logaras the headlands and bays diverge a little from the road and become less crowded. Here and there tents have been set up where sand has drifted over the rocky platforms or where trees provide a little shade. After Logaras are the pocket-sized beaches of **Pounda** (not to be confused with the little port of Pounda on the west coast), **Mezadha** and **Tzirdakia** but nowhere is there isolation.

If the coastline is followed farther then it opens out into the broad sandy bay backed by a swathe of green that is **Chrisi Akti** (Golden Sands), another popular stop on the bus route. This, in turn, gives way to the terminus at **Drios** with its little cluster of shops, hotels and apartments. A little concrete lane zig-zags down to the shore from the bus terminus and finishes alongside an isolated antiquity on the pebbles and rock outcrops of the shore. Here the rocky platform has been excavated into a series of shallow parallel trenches called *neosiki*. These are believed to have been the stocks into which the ships were drawn by early boatmakers for repair. They may even have been the original maker's slipways.

Drios is the end of the line for those whose travel is undertaken by bus. To venture further the simplest method is to hire a moped or motor cycle, of which a variety are available, at the agents beside the bus stop. The same company stores another set for hire in the unlikely location of an old bus parked at the roadside between Piso Livadi and Marpissa, close to the official camp site. Apart from walking, this is the only available means of transport but it is a fairly arduous business owing to the vagaries of the road. The reasonable metalled surface comes to an end just beyond Drios and is replaced by a dirt track packed with loose stones and rock outcrops. This is dusty in summer and speed is controlled by the need to circumnavigate the occasional hazards of the highway. It

Cycladic chimneys near Angeria.

is, nevertheless, worth the effort.

The road does not follow the shoreline closely, partly because of the bays and headlands, which would make the route long and sinuous, and partly because valleys dissect the hillslopes and these are at their deepest near the shore. Farther up the hill, away from the coast, it has been possible to engineer the way, if that is a valid phrase, without a switchback of ups and downs. A few little tracks lead down to the sea from the road and it is these diversions that are likely to provide most interest, especially as only a limited number of people are going to do likewise.

A cape, **Akrotiri Pyrgos,** juts out into the Aegean south of Drios and beyond it a red earth track leads down to the coast at **Glyfa.** It ultimately opens out on to a stony but attractive little bay but just above it a farm provides ice cold drinks to those making the journey. Many of the buildings on this southern side of Paros are old and display the distinctive features of Cycladic architecture. This farm is one such structure though additions and modernisation to entice the visitor have modified its form. Chickens scrabble about on the road which passes through the farm. On one side the buildings have one of many local designs of chimney in which the top is covered by a white dome or slab of stone so that the smoke emerges from apertures in the four sides. On the other side of the track a vine covered loggia stands beside one of the many dovecotes dispersed across Paros. It has a square tower with little crowned turrets on the corners. The walls are pierced between narrow tile ledges on which the doves line up and look down on the rustling olive trees.

Glyfa is a pleasant spot but the track leads nowhere and steps must be retraced up the hill to the road. Nearby, on the landward side, another little track leads up to a farm building which gives access to the very curious little chapel of **Agios Ioannis Spiliotis** (St John of the Cave). This church is indeed constructed in a cave within the hillside and is approached down a short passage. Once again its structure embodies marble pieces of an earlier age.

Two more kilometres on the execrable road and it swings westward in the direction of Alyki. The juniper covered slopes fall gently away to a coast of small bays and capes and the offshore archipelago of small islets. Beyond, in the hazy Aegean light, the rounded hills of Antiparos form the background.

The road here is rough and relatively straight but the coast bows outward becoming less accessible in consequence until the road approaches it three kilometres on. There are a few buildings constituting the hamlet of **Trypiti** but the shoreline has not been

Trypiti cove.

developed. A steep little track with a bare rock surface in places descends to the shore between stone walls. It is not suitable even for motor cycles but a diversion on foot can be interesting.

There are sandy bays for those seeking them at the northern end of this section of coast in the direction of Alyki. Elsewhere the shore has rock outcrops in some places and massive rounded boulders in others. White marble slabs dip into the sea along part of the beach. Erosion has prised blocks from these strata and waves have rolled them back and forth to form the massive cobbles. A layer of horizontal breccia comprised of partly cemented angular debris sits uncomfortably across the truncated and tilted marble strata. These stony beds thicken in places towards the southeast at Akrotiri Mavros. The material is not well lithified so that waves are able to attack the base at the low cliffs, undercutting them and excavating a series of holes and small caves. The name Trypiti is derived from the Greek word *trypa* meaning hole.

Agriculturally, this area is stony and fairly barren, providing some olives, a little grain and pasture for goats and sheep. At one point on the coast is evidence of an alternative resource, used in the past. A little pile of alien black rock fragments rests on the white marble. On investigation this is seen to be a slightly blue-black colour and is fairly dense. Some pieces show patches of pink to prove conclusively that these are ores of manganese consisting of the black oxide, pyrolusite, and the pink carbonate, rhodonite.

Angeria village marks the end of this wild section of coast. It is clean and white and is set up on a small hill. It also marks the unexpected and welcome appearance of a concrete road leading down to the coast at Alyki. In the opposite direction a dirt road climbs steeply and tortuously for nearly three kilometres to the active nunnery of **Agioi Theodoroi,** where the inmates earn a living by spinning and weaving. The building is modern but their ways are old and they even follow the old Orthodox calendar which is out of synchronisation with the current system. They are, nevertheless, prepared to accept modern visitors, as in most monasteries, provided they dress with decorum displaying neither legs, arms nor bodies. The merit of a journey such as this lies not only in attaining the objective but in the journey itself, which provides fine views down to Alyki and over to Antiparos.

Alyki is a watering place. It is modern and consists to a large degree of apartments and rooms to let for the influx of Athenians in summer. Building is in progress all round, noisily on the harbour installations, dustily on the roads, and hopefully at the nearby new airport. The little bay is shallow and sandy and made for children

Alyki, a tamarisk shaded restaurant by the beach.

but one of the most pleasant prospects is a fish meal in the tamarisk-shaded restaurant whose white-walled patio curves out on to the sand.

North of Alyki lies the broad gently sloping plain which stretches out to Paroikia and approaches the Antiparos narrows. The little ferry terminal at **Pounda** is visible over a long distance on the coast beyond the fine beach of **Voutakos.** Inland from Pounda two attractions to travellers are the Butterfly Valley at **Petaloudes** where one species is attracted to the leaves in numbers almost equalled by the donkeymen and their captive tourists. The idea, no doubt, has caught on from the similar and better known Butterfly Valley on Rhodes.

A perhaps more attractive prospect nearby is the ridge which extends from Petaloudes northeastwards in the direction of Paroikia. Rather than endure the dubious delights of donkey transport, you can use the local bus service from Paroikia to Alyki to approach both Butterfly Valley and the ridge route which leads to the attractive site of the monastery of **Christou Dasous** (Christ of the Forest), which lies near the crest of the ridge. The monastery is famed on Paros as the burial place of the revered Saint Arsenios but it also commands fine views over a wide span of the coast including Paroikia itself.

Paros and Naxos are not unchanged or unchanging but they possess much that is unique and they are essentially Greek. The massive hotels, casinos, shopping arcades and cars of Spanish, French and Italian resorts are fortunately absent. Tales of Mediterranean pollution are seen as mere fables in the isolation of the Aegean. The wine dark sea sparkles as it ever did and its islands provide an inexhaustible source of interest and enjoyment for holidaymaker and Hellenophile alike. One journey will not satiate nor, indeed will ten. *Kalo Taxidi,* good journey!

Accommodation

Hotels on Paros

Class	Name	Location	Beds	Tel. (code 0284)
B	Aegeon	Paroikia	45	22153/4
B	Arian	Paroikia	16	21490
B	Dilion	Paroikia	27	21479
B	Xenia	Paroikia	44	21394
C	Alkyon	Paroikia	46	21506
C	Argo	Paroikia	83	21367
C	Argonautis	Paroikia	27	21440
C	Asterias	Paroikia	50	21797
C	Galinos	Paroikia	65	21480
C	Georgy	Paroikia	43	21667
C	Hermes	Paroikia	36	21217
C	Loisa	Paroikia	22	21480
C	Paros	Paroikia	22	21319
C	Stela	Paroikia	38	21502
C	Zannet	Paroikia	15	—
B	Hippocambus	Naoussa	94	51223/4
B	Naoussa	Naoussa	19	51207
C	Alibrantis	Naoussa	29	—
C	Ambelas	Naoussa	32	51324
C	Atlantis	Naoussa	40	51209
C	Calypso	Naoussa	46	51488
C	Cavos	Naoussa	25	51367
C	Galini	Naoussa	22	51210
C	Mary	Naoussa	66	51249
C	Minoa	Naoussa	51	51309
C	Piperi	Naoussa	16	51295
B	Aphroditi	Alyki	40	21489
C	Angeliki	Alyki	26	21244
C	Annezina	Drios	26	41364
C	Aura	Drios	18	41249
C	Julia	Drios	23	41249
C	Ivi	Drios	23	41249
B	Xenia	Lefkes	28	71248
C	Logaras	Marpissa	16	41389

Class	Name	Location	Beds	Tel. (code 0284)
B	Andromachi	Piso Livadi	11	41387
B	Marpissa	Piso Livadi	21	41288
C	Leto	Piso Livadi	28	41283
C	Lodos	Piso Livadi	20	41218
C	Piso Livadi	Piso Livadi	24	41309
C	Vicky	Piso Livadi	28	41333

Eating out

Restaurants in Paroikia

Parostia Located a short distance from the harbour and the central square, Plateia Ethnikis Antistasis, on the side road Odos Lochagou Gravari. The Parostia is in a most attractive garden setting with tables grouped around a date palm and surrounded by bougainvillea and hibiscus. The restaurant offers a quality European menu including a variety of veal dishes at less than 500 drachmae.

To Tamarisko Near to the Parostia through an arch into Odos Agokarito. A vine loggia with suspended basket lights, a spreading palm and an enclosing stone wall provides a venue and a menu comparable to any.

O Kyriakos In contrast, along the Odos Lochagou beyond the Mavrogeni fountain is the Kyriakos taverna with roadside tables beneath the trees, where you can enjoy simple lamb, veal and chicken dishes at about 300 drachmae.

Levantis A little more distant from the harbour along the central shopping street, Odos Lochagou Fokianou, where it is joined from the right by Odos Archilochou, is Levantis restaurant. White walls with a cane and vine loggia provide deep shade. Dishes such as octopus stifado, beef sautéd with green olives and pork in mustard sauce cost between 400 and 500 drachmae.

May Tey For those seeking a change from Greek and European fare, the May Tey, on Archilochou street provides a variety of oriental dishes.

Balcony Bistro The main street opens out at another of Mavrogeni's fountains beneath a spray of flaming hibiscus on the chapel of Agia Trias. Overlooking this is the Balcony Bistro serving a variety of crêpes between 200 and 300 drachmae and dishes such as marinated sesame chicken and pasta carbonara for little over 400 drachmae.

Kyriako's Restaurant Adjacent to the Balcony, Kyriako's provides cool refined conditions and an extensive European menu. Recommended is its variety of steaks between 450 and 750 drachmae, also the Fisherman's Plate at 650 drachmae.

Hibiscus Restaurant Close to Kyriako's on the waterfront is the little square of Plateia Frangiskou Veledza. Large dense shady trees provide the canopy for this restaurant specialising in fish dishes such as lobster and swordfish kebabs. Among other items lamb Giovetsi is recommended.

Corfo Leon A little square known as Plateia Nikolaos Mavrogenis lies between the Hibiscus and the central windmill. Here the Corfo Leon has round wood tables and a solitary shade tree and offers simple traditional Greek dishes. It is surrounded by small eating places such as the **Pierrot le Fou** crêperie bistro offering dishes between 170 and 370 drachmae.

Aligaria On the quiet little square of Frangiskou Tsantana, the Aligaria serves Greek dishes such as squid, mullet, snapper, souvlaki and dolmades with good service and the lowest prices. Almost adjacent, the **Dimitris** provides similar fare.

Paroikia is a very busy place, though perhaps not yet in the same league as Mykonos town. In consequence it is not only well supplied with traditional Greek and international restaurants, but also with a large number of fast food premises. Many of these are located around the central square. They are very popular and include the **Palm Tree,** the **Argonauta** and, beside the mill, **Apostolopouli.** Others are along the length of the waterfront with its little squares. Towards the bus station are the **Oasis** and **Angelo's** and, in the opposite direction, **Babby's Pizza** and **Spaghetti House** and the **Specialistas** Restaurant with its western breakfasts.

There are bars in plenty. Where Odos Archilochou reaches the waterfront is the raised balcony of **Pebble Bar** with its pleasant outlook over the bay. **Oscar's** is nearby on Archilochou. On the main shopping street, Lochagou Fokianou, close to the Mavrogeni fountain and Agia Trias and Agia Paraskevi is the **Pirate** cocktail bar with its jazz and the **Apollon** garden bar with a background of Greek classical music.

Naoussa

Naoussa is the second largest settlement on Paros and its rapid growth has been matched by development of restaurants and coffee bars. There are two areas in which amenities are concentrated, namely around the little harbour and along the high street. Undoubtedly the harbour offers the most attractive prospect where every property looks out across the crowded caiques.

Limanaki The largest restaurant overlooking the head of the harbour with tables inside and on the water's edge. Pleasant for a midday fish lunch, a cool drink in the heat of the day or a wide variety of fish and meat dishes in the evening.

Mouragio Taverna Backs on to the little harbour but also looks out on to the jetty for small passenger vessels to the beaches. A very popular place for traditional Greek dishes, especially fish.

I Stasis Ouzeri Tables extend along the harbour side of the chapel. It is an experience and a pleasure to sample the ouzo and to tackle the huge mackerel which have been split and baked, first in the sun and then on the grill.

To Naftikon Ouzeri A small charcoal grill beside the harbour square draped with the octopi for which it is famous.

Also around the harbour are the small **Diva Restaurant,** the **Malamos** and **Kastello** snack bars, and the **Remezzo, Chez Linardo, Barbarossa** and **Labyrinth** bars. The latter is notable for its selection of fruit and vegetable juices.

Restaurants stretch out up the hill along the high street from the sea. On one side the **Europe Restaurant** and the **Varaos** offer a varied menu and competent presentation. On the other the **Glaros kafeneion** is an ideal self service breakfast place almost adjacent to **Angela's** and the **Panais** taverna. The problem here is that the crowds of people tax the resources of the restaurants. Long delays in the evening are almost inevitable and the ambience is not improved by a makeshift shooting gallery and a 'Game of Chance' stall.

Table 17   Ferries from Paroikia operating in most weather conditions

Vessel	Monday	Tuesday	Wednesday	Thursday	Friday	Saturday	Sunday
Lemnos	Piraeus (d.12.15)	Ios Santorini (d.13.15) Piraeus (d.22.45)	Naxos Ios Santorini Heraklion (d.13.15)	Piraeus (d.12.15)	Naxos Ios Sikinos Folegandros Santorini Heraklion (d.14.15)	Syros Piraeus (d.14.15)	Naxos Ios Santorini Heraklion (d.13.15)
Naxos		Naxos (d.13.30) Piraeus (d.22.30)	Naxos (d.13.30) Piraeus (d.22.30)	Naxos (d.13.30) Piraeus (d.22.30)	Naxos (d.13.30) Piraeus (d.22.30)	Naxos (d.13.30) Piraeus (d.22.30)	Naxos (d.13.30) Piraeus (d.22.30)
Aigaion	Ikaria Samos (d.02.00) Piraeus (d.16.45)	Ikaria Samos (d.13.30)	Piraeus (d.13.30)	Ikaria Samos (d.13.30)	Piraeus (d.13.30)	Ikaria Samos (d.13.30)	Piraeus (d.13.30)

Nereus	Amorgos Astypalea Rhodes (d.24.00)	Amorgos Astypalea Kalymnos Kos Nissiros Tilos Symi Rhodes (d.23.30)				Piraeus (d.05.00) · Naxos Donoussa Koufonissia Amorgos Astypalea (d.22.35)	Syros Piraeus (d.22.00)
Nissos Chios		Naxos (d.04.00) · Piraeus (d.10.45)			Naxos (d.0400) · Piraeus (d.10.45)		
Santorini	Ios Santorini (d.14.00) · Piraeus (d.23.00)	Naxos Ios Sikinos · Folegandros Santorini (d.15.00)	Syros Piraeus (d.14.00)	Ios Santorini (d.14.00) · Piraeus (d.23.00)	Ios Santorini (d.14.00) · Piraeus (d.23.00)	Ios Santorini (d.14.00) · Piraeus (d.23.00)	Ios Santorini (d.14.00) · Piraeus (d.23.00)

Table 17 continued

Vessel	Monday	Tuesday	Wednesday	Thursday	Friday	Saturday	Sunday
Atlas II		Naxos (d.04.00) Syros Rafina (d.14.00)		Naxos (d.04.00) Syros Rafina (d.14.00)			
Giorgios Express	Folegandros Sikinos Ios Santorini (d.02.00)		Naxos Ios Santorini (d.13.15)	Naxos Ios Santorini (d.13.15)	Ios Santorini (d.24.00)	Piraeus (d.13.00)	Piraeus (d.13.00)
	Syros Piraeus (d.14.00)		Piraeus (d.23.30)	Piraeus (d.23.30)		Naxos Ios Santorini (d.24.00)	

Vessel	Monday	Tuesday	Wednesday	Thursday	Friday	Saturday	Sunday
Ios	Naxos Mykonos (d.11.45)	Naxos Mykonos (d.11.45)	Naxos Mykonos (d.11.45)	Naxos Mykonos (d.11.45)	Naxos Mykonos (d.11.45)	Naxos Mykonos (d.11.45)	Naxos Mykonos (d.11.45)
	Ios Santorini (d.18.15)	Ios Santorini (d.18.15)	Ios Santorini (d.18.15)	Ios Santorini (d.18.15)	Ios Santorini (d.18.15)	Ios Santorini (d.18.15)	Ios Santorini (d.18.15)
Megalochari	Ios Santorini (d.11.25)	Ios Santorini (d.11.25)	Ios Santorini (d.11.25)	Ios Santorini (d.11.25)	Ios Santorini (d.11.25)	Ios Santorini (d.11.25)	Mykonos Tinos (d.13.15)
	Tinos (d.20.00)	Tinos (d.20.00)	Tinos (d.20.00)	Tinos (d.20.00)	Tinos (d.20.00)	Tinos (d.20.00)	
Latsos II		Sifnos (d.11.00)	Sifnos (d.11.00)	Sifnos (d.11.00)	Sifnos (d.11.00)	Sifnos (d.11.00)	Sifnos (d.11.00)
		Naxos (d.17.30)	Naxos (d.17.30)	Naxos (d.17.30)	Naxos (d.17.30)	Naxos (d.17.30)	Naxos (d.17.30)

Table 18 Ferries from Paroikia which are subject to weather conditions

(There are daily ferry excursions from Naoussa at 08.30 to Delos-Mykonos and also to Naxos. On Wednesday the *Daphne II* sails from Piso Livadi at a similar time.)

185

TWELVE

Antiparos

The island of Antiparos is separated by a channel 1.2 km wide from the southwest side of Paros. It is 12 km long and spindle shaped, tapering to north and south. It is a quiet place, accessible, and worth a visit especially for those seeking relief from the whirlwind that is Paroikia in summer.

There are two ways of approaching Antiparos. The most popular, by far, is by one of the small ferries that ply from the jetty in the centre of Paroikia, a sail of about 7 km. On a good day this is pleasant as the vessel threads its way through steeply outcropping granite rocks, Kokkinos Tourlos and Mavros Tourlos and the islets of Saliagos and Strogylonisi. The former was the site of a Neolithic settlement of fishermen at a time when Paros is believed to have been linked to Antiparos by a causeway. Certainly the channel is very shallow being only a few metres deep at any point. The problem with following this route to Antiparos is in windy conditions. The ferries are whisked on their way by a following wind but have to fight against the waves and the spray on the return journey.

The alternative route is to take the bus from the waterfront terminal in Paroikia to Pounda, not such a regular service as that to Naoussa or across the island to Piso Livadi. (The tarmac road passes on the way a path leading down to the enclosed little bay at Agia Eirini, another place which may justify a visit. It has a little church of the same name, a sandy beach shaded by tamarisk trees, a restaurant and a camp site.) When the bus reaches Pounda, it is the end of the road with a handful of houses, a church and, nearby, a small holiday hotel. Pounda looks out across the channel at its narrowest point to the village of Antiparos or, as it is also known, Kastro. A tiny ferry connects the two places at hourly intervals, unless there is a special demand or a number of people are waiting for transport. Small though it is, the ferry has an enclosed cabin, providing shelter as it runs broadside on to the waves as it crosses the narrows.

Antiparos town and environs

Antiparos town lies on the east coast of the island near to the northern point of its spindle shape. Its harbour is a sheltered bay connected by a road cutting across the northern peninsula to a similar bay on the western side. This bay possesses one of the island's best beaches, **Siphnaikos Yialos.** On the roads almost inevitably, a Venetian castle was constructed in the mid-15th century in order to protect farmers from piratical and Turkish raids. The castle's rectangular form and square inner courtyard are still clearly discernible although later dwellings have been attached to the walls and the original central round tower has been largely erased.

The waterfront of Antiparos has some modern hotels and apartments along its outer margins. The centre, where the main road begins, lies in the shade of tamarisks. A 'fast food' self-service cafe provides breakfast there and its tables benefit from the grey green fronds of the trees. Pleasant restaurants are grouped around this focus of the harbour which is also the terminus for small tourist ferries to Paroikia and to the cave of Antiparos. From here also departs the solitary small bus which serves the island and its community of visitors.

The native population of Antiparos is small, numbering fewer than six hundred, most of whom live in the town. There are, in addition, the summer residents, some of whom are Athenians with houses in or near the town while others are the foreign visitors seeking quietness, Many of these stay in the camp site at the northern tip of Antiparos where it is sheltered by the offshore island of Dipla. Here there are trees for shade, sandy beaches and, as the advertisers are keen to impress, 'bare brown bodies from top to toe, free from all clothes, worries and woe'. In addition to temporary residents, Antiparos has its minor daily flood of visitors coming over from Paroikia by boat.

The cave

For most, the principal object of the visit is Antiparos cave, supposedly one of the most famous and attractive sites in Greece. Certainly there is a Greek dimension to this cave which makes it a little unique but not necessarily everything that is Greek is good even to the most avid Hellenophile, and the merits of this cave should be considered before the visit is undertaken.

The location of the cave is at a height of over 200 metres on a site over half way down the length of the island. The base of the hill in which it is found can be approached by boats from Paroikia and Antiparos or by the tiny bus which wends its way along the rough dirt road following the east side of the island's hills. The bus makes the journey several times a day leaving its passengers at the intersection with the track scaling the hill to the cave. Nearby is the jetty on which sea passengers are unloaded. In either case a posse of donkeys and controllers lie in wait like vultures contemplating descent on to helpless prey.

Novices in Greek travel will not have met the breed of Greek donkeymen and their charges. They are found in many places attempting to provide transportation up steep slopes such as the climb to the town of Santorini from the harbour, and to the Acropolis at Lindos on Rhodes. As a group they are earthily attractive with wrinkled sunburned faces, flat caps, bulging corporations over leather belts, and knotted cotton scarves. They also have, no matter what their age or shape, an enviable store of energy with which to climb endlessly up and down hills. On the other hand, they have qualities akin to those of Athenian taxi drivers when it comes to enticing customers and arranging a suitable price for their transport. Those with the energy to go it alone may get more pleasure out of watching the antics of others on the ascent.

The climb is not difficult. It is a dirt track through the grey and green vegetation which covers the rounded hills of Antiparos. The slope is rather concave so that it becomes a little steeper at higher levels. Some tens of metres short of the crest of the hills is the entrance to the cave with a courtyard surrounded by a stone wall. Within this enclosure lies the little chapel of **Agios Ioannis Spiliotis** (St John of the Cave) which dates from 1774.

The visible entrance to the cave is a broad wedge-shaped aperture underneath a massive stratum of inclined limestone. Rainwater, seeping down through the joints in this overlying stratum, has been responsible for dissolving the lime along strata bedding planes to form the chain of caverns. The same carbon-dioxide-rich waters which have dissolved the lime in some places have been responsible for depositing it in others, with the assistance of contained algae. These precipitates take the form of fluted sheets, stalagmites and stalactites. The Greek term for the cave is **Spileo Stalaktiton.**

Within the outer entrance to the cave one huge stalactite extends from roof to floor like a massive supporting pillar. On one side of it steps lead down to an iron bar gate which is opened at 10 am by the keeper. He first sets the oil-fired generator into noisy and smoky action and then collects the fee and issues tickets to waiting visitors. No attempt is made to explain, guide or draw attention to any phenomena.

It might be said with some justification that when you have seen one cave you have seen them all. All are associated with limestones and the mechanics of their formation does not vary greatly. Similarly the products of precipitation are broadly similar. Only the details and the scale are variable. In the cave of Antiparos the scale is no greater than many others in Europe and the details which add so much to the charm are unfortunately inferior.

The tragedy about Antiparos cave is that it has been vandalised over a very long period of time. Officers of the Russian fleet which was based in Naoussa Bay during the 1770s were reported to have visited the cave, breaking off stalactites and returning with them to Russia. Other deposits were shattered by gunfire and grenades during the Second World War, supposedly in the search for escaped prisoners. Unescorted tourists also have been responsible for the removal of accessible trophies. It is possible for them to roam unchecked even now through the wet and dripping galleries.

Incomplete pinnacles and pillars spoil the perfection of the cave but far worse is the vast amount of graffiti daubing every rippled wall deposit and ribbed pillar. Some are modern marks implanted by knife and felt pen but others are old and lengthy writings along the stalagmites. It is one gigantic autograph book featuring, among many, the Marquis de Nointel, French Ambassador to the Ottoman Empire in 1673, who is said to have held a Christmas Midnight Mass there. The first King of Greece, Otto, left his mark in 1840 and even the supreme Hellenophile, Lord Byron, who should have known better, is reputed to have succumbed. Short of indulging in the dubious pleasure of searching through the myriads of marks it is impossible to sort out fact from fiction. What is certain is that the Antiparos cave has been spoiled in a way that is not true of other similar European wonders. At least the early cave men were artistic. More recently, egotistical scribblers have taken over.

Agios Georgios

It is pleasant to emerge from the cave to climb up to the top of the ridge where the limestone forms a very sparse and patchy pavement between the spiny tufts. Though the views are commonly hazy and this is not quite the highest point on the island, it is a solitary and peaceful place. The few dwellings are evident and so, too, is the church crowning the highest point Profitis Ilias at 307 metres.

Outside the immediate environs of the town of Antiparos, the island is unspoiled and without amenities. The solitude can be judged from the fact that a mobile shop trundles along the dusty road to the cave path to serve the parched visitors on their descent. Access to the quiet stretches of coastline and to small sandy strands is obtained by walking or by the use of the little bus. Just twice a day — once on its first journey — this travels not simply to the cave but to the southwest corner of the island at **Agios Georgios** in an area of total solitude overlooking the little channel separating Antiparos from the deserted island of Despotiko. The bus returns in late afternoon to the same spot to pick up those who have returned to explore this remote but pleasant corner.

Accommodation

Hotel on Antiparos

Class	Name	Location	Beds	Tel. (code 0284)
C	Chryssi Akti	Antiparos	17	61206